MUSLIM EDUCATIONAL THOUGHT IN THE MIDDLE AGES

MUSLIM EDUCATIONAL THOUGHT IN THE MIDDLE AGES

Dr. S.M. Ziauddin Alavi

ATLANTIC PUBLISHERS & DISTRIBUTORS
4215/1, Ansari Road, Darya Ganj
New Delhi-110002

Published by :
Atlantic Publishers & Distributors
4215/1, Ansari Road, Darya Ganj,
New Delhi-110002

Head Office :
B-2, Vishal Enclave, Najafgarh Road,
New Delhi-110027
Phone : 5413460

Printed at : Devendra Printers through Chawla Composers,
Delhi

FOREWORD

I am pleased to write a Foreword to Dr. Alavi's present treatise on Muslim Educational Thought in the Middle Ages. It is an exhaustive study of the Islamic contribution to education in the Middle Ages, along with historical background of the development of the education.

The present work deals with the philosophical concepts of the Quran and the terms like Reality, Knowledge, Worship of God etc. which have been discussed from their philosophical perspective. The Muslim educational thought has been analysed in the light of different schools of philosophy. The philosophy of Plato, Aristotle and other philosophers has been also touched with the objective to trace the extent of their influence over Arab Philosophers.

The eminent Muslim Philosophers like Ibn Sina, Ibn Miskawaih, al-Ghazzali and Ibn Rushd have made valuable contribution to the promotion of Muslim education and Islamic jurisprudence. The concepts and ideas evolved by them have been critically examined with their impact upon the Muslim education in the Islamic civilisation.

The author has given a brief account of the aims, contents, methodology of teaching and organisation of the Muslim education. The courses of study, methods of teaching and status of a teacher are most important components of every system of education. The author has made an in-depth study of all these concepts and has presented them in a lucid manner.

I wish and hope this treatise shall prove helpful to the student and the general reader.

MUSHIRUL HAQ

FOREWORD

I am pleased to write a [illegible] to [illegible] study [illegible] Muslim [illegible] Theories in the Middle Ages [illegible] an [illegible] study of the [illegible] contribution to education in the Middle Ages [illegible] of the development of [illegible] education.

[illegible] present work [illegible] the philosophical concepts [illegible] and the [illegible] knowledge [illegible] been [illegible] philosophical [illegible] The philosophy of Plato, Aristotle and [illegible] philosophy has been [illegible] with the [illegible] influence of Arab philosophy.

[illegible] have made valuable contribution to the [illegible] of Muslim [illegible] Islamic [illegible] The concepts and ideas evolved [illegible] upon the Muslim [illegible].

The author has given a brief account of the [illegible] of [illegible] of the Muslim [illegible] education [illegible] the [illegible] of education. The author has made [illegible] of these [illegible] of [illegible].

I wish and hope this [illegible] useful [illegible] the general reader.

PREFACE

The Islamic contribution to education in the Middle Ages has been neglected by the Muslim scholars as well as the Orientalists. There are no doubt lots of papers on the subject but there is dearth of books dealing with the various aspects of the subject with the result that there are many misconceptions about the aim, content and the role of Muslim education, such as the view that the Muslim education was simply religious and aimed at producing religious scholars who were good for nothing or that it was because of this out-dated education that Muslim society of the later Middle Ages became backward. The aim of the book is to remove such ideas from the minds of the people by presenting the Muslim education of the Middle Ages in the right perspective and by bringing to light the educational ideas of Muslim educators like al-Ghazzālī, Ibn Miskawaih, Ibn Sīna and Ibn Khaldun and a host of other educators. It is also pointed out that it was this system of education which produced savants like al-Berunī (Mathematician-Astronomer), al-Mas'ūdī (Historian), Ibn Yunus (Astronomer), al-Khwarizmī (Astronomer), Ibn Hazm (Physicist) and philosophers whose names are too well known to be recounted here. If the present book succeeds in bringing about a better understanding of the Muslim education as a whole it will be a great service to the cause of Islam and to the culture and civilisation of the Medieval period which was the direct outcome of the Islamic system of education.

An attempt has also been made to trace the development of Islamic education system from the rise of Islam upto the 14th century in its philosophical and religious setting and to examine critically the contribution of the Muslim scholars and philosophers to education in all its varied aspects.

The study comprises nine chapters dealing with various aspects of Islamic education.

The first chapter outlines the development of education in its historical perspective. For this purpose the period has been divided into five heads *viz.* education under the prophet and the pious caliphs, education under Umayyads, education under early Abbasids, education under later Abbasids and the disintegration of the empire. The characteristic features of the education system have been discussed in detail. In addition to this a glimpse of the education system in Spain and India is also to be found in this chapter.

The second chapter deals with the philosophical concepts of the Qur'ān such as Reality, Knowledge, Worship of God etc. which serve as the foundation of education. In the light of these concepts is discussed the Islamic concept of nature of man and the nature of knowledge purporting to show that the tenets of Islam are in keeping with human nature and that the noblest knowledge is the knowledge of the Qur'ān and Ḥadīth. It has also been pointed out that in Islam there is no restriction on the study of sciences dealing with worldly affairs.

The third chapter is devoted to an analytical study of the schools of philosophy which influenced Muslim educational thought. As the Muslim philosophers drew inspiration and guidance from Greek philosophers the study is preceded by a description of basic concepts of Plato, Aristotle and the neo-Platonists. The aim is to show how far the Arab philosophers were influenced by these philosophers. This is followed by the study of the basic philosophical concepts of some Muslim philosophers like a-Fārābī, Ibn Sīna, Ibn Miskawaih, al-Ghazzālī and Ibn Rushd. The common characteristic of these philosophers was that they tried to harmonise Greek philosophy with the tenets of Islam. Al-Ghazzālī was the only exception who thought that the fundamentals of Islam cannot and should not be harmonised with Greek philosophy. In addition to this attention is also directed towards the philosophical movements such as Mu'tazilism, Ash'arism and Ikhwan on the one hand and the theologians and Ṣufism on the other as great forces influencing Muslim educational thought and giving a variegated pattern to Muslim education.

Chapters IV to VI are devoted to the study of the educational philosophy of some eminent philosophers and educationists such as Ibn Miskawaih, al-G͟hazzālī and Ibn K͟haldūn. The most important of these philosophers was al-G͟hazzālī who wielded great influence on Muslim education from 12th to 14th century onwards. Al-G͟hazzālī propounded the theory that education should be nothing but religious and moral in character. Ibn K͟haldūn who came about 200 years afterwards pointed out the snags of the education system in vogue in the Islamic countries. He wanted to rectify these defects and at the same time gave a sociological orientation to education while retain its religious character. He broke new ground in methodology of teaching and emphasised greater intellectual effort on the part of the pupils.

Chapter VII presents the educational ideas of some more educational thinkers like al-Fārābī, Ibn Sīna, Ibn Suhnūn, Ibn al Ḥajj and al-Zarnujī.

Chapter VIII is devoted to a synoptic view of the aims, content, methodology and organisation of Muslim education. The aims of education were formulated in the light of the teachings of the Qur'ān and Ḥadīt͟h. Hence the most important aim of education was to instil in the minds of the pupils the beliefs and ideals for which Islam stands. The courses of studies were of two types—one under the influence of Arab philosophers and the other prepared by theologians. In the former type of courses the emphasis was on philosophical interpretation of the tenets of Islam. The courses included philosophy in all its varied branches but Qur'ān and Ḥadīt͟h also formed part of the curriculum. In the second group Qur'ān and Ḥadīt͟h and related subjects were studied in greater depth. In addition to this Astronomy, Rhetories ('Ilm Kalām), philology were also taught. The method of teaching generally followed was reading from the text or lecture by the teacher. There was little scope for pupil's participation in the teaching-learning process. Rote learning was stressed. Reform of the method of teaching was attempted by scholars like al-G͟hazzālī and Ibn K͟haldūn. As regards organisation of education the topics discussed include organisation of teaching work, status of teachers, duties and responsibilities of teachers and students, the examination system, granting of degrees and certificates etc.

The last chapter gives a brief resume of the outstanding elements of the education system in the Islamic countries in the Middle Ages. An attempt has also been made to assess the influence of Muslim philosophers and educators on Western educational thought and on the revival of learning in Europe. This is followed by a critical examination of the education system of the Muslims as well as to dispelling some misconceptions about the role of Muslim education in the Middle Ages. Lastly the relevance of Muslim educational thought for the Muslims of today has been discussed.

In the end the writer wishes to express his gratitude to Prof. Mushirul Haq for writing the Foreword.

S.M.Z. Alavi

CONTENTS

CONTENTS

CHAPTER I

AN OUTLINE OF DEVELOPMENT OF EDUCATION IN THE ISLAMIC WORLD FROM 7TH TO 14TH CENTURIES

The period under study is spread over seven hundred years from the rise of Islam to the times of Ibn Khaldūn. The period witnessed many vicissitudes political, religious as well as educational. During the days of the prophet and the pious caliphs education was conducted strictly in line with the philosophy of education and life as enunciated in the Qur'ān. The Umayyads paid only lip service to the Islamic ideals. The early Abbasids popularised Greek sciences and philosophy at the cost of Islamic ideals. The later Abbasids reversed the policies of their predecessors and persecuted those who subscribed to Greek ideas. But by this time the Abbasid power was weakened and the empire was dismembered and small principalities rose which extended support to their own sectarian ideologies. All these factors were responsible for shaping the educational thought during the period. For a detailed study of all these factors the whole period is divided into six parts: (i) Education during the life of the prophet and the pious caliphs; (ii) Education under the Umayyads; (iii) Education under early Abbasids; (iv) Education under later Abbasids and the break up of the empire; (v) Education in Spain; (vi) Education in India.

(i) *Education during the life of the Prophet and the pious Caliphs*: The prophet himself was the teacher, he taught the Qur'ān to the companions and explained the significance of the Quranic *Āyāt* and guided them to lead the life of a true

Muslim according to the behest of the Qur'ān. The prophet listened to their problems religious as well as domestic and solved them with divine knowledge. The Masjid Nabawi served as the place of instruction. The Muslims thronged to the mosque at the time of prayers and at odd hours to seek guidance from the prophet. The prophet used to appoint teachers for teaching, reading and writing who taught in various mosques of Medina. 'Ubaid-ibn al-Sāmit says that the prophet appointed him as a teacher in the school of Suffah (in Medina) for teaching Qur'ān. Suffah was connected with the mosque of the prophet in Medina. This place was set apart for lodging of newcomers and those who were too poor to have a house of their own. This was a regular residential school where reading, writing, Muslim law, memorising of Qur'ān and methods of reciting Qur'ān correctly were taught under the direct supervision of the prophet. The despatch of teachers to newly converted tribes was regular feature of the educational policy of the prophet. Suffah was not the only school at Medina. There were about nine mosques in Medina at the time of the prophet each one of them served as a school for the teaching of the Qur'ān. The subjects of studies included beside the study of the Qur'ān and Ḥadīth, elementary mathematics, rudiments of medicine, astronomy, geneology and phonetics.[1]

After the death of the prophet his companions followed the same practice of teaching in mosques. The pious caliphs sent teachers of the Qur'ān to various countries under Muslim rule. These teachers delivered lectures on religious matters and taught the Qur'ān. Some of the students learnt the Qur'ān by heart. Thus the education system in those days acknowledged the Qur'ān as the core and the pivot of learning.

(ii) *Education under the Umayyads* : The Umayyads were described by some Orientalists as more secular than religious and more Arab than Muslim in Character.[2] In many respects they reverted to the sentiments of pre-Islamic days and violated Islamic ideals. In the education of the princes emphasis was laid on poetry and history. The Qur'ān also formed part of their studies. During this period there were two complimentary streams of courses. Firstly the purely religious courses comprising the Qur'ān. Ḥadīth and Arabic language. Secondly there were courses which emphasised Arabic language and poetry. The education system of the Umayyads was also influenced by the fact that Greek works on Alchemy, Medicine and Astronomy were translated into Arabic by the order of Khālid bin Yazīd. This modest beginning of translation work heralded a great movement which influenced Muslim thought. This period also saw the rise of many schools of religion such as the Shiites and the Kharijites who had their own education systems. The mosques continued to be centre of religious learning but sometimes served as centres of higher learning in language and literature. During this period another type of school came into existence *viz.* the Kuttāb in which education was imparted to children in the Qur'ān and the Ḥadīth.

(iii) *Education under early Abbasids* : The early Abbasid period was marked by translation of scientific and philosophical works from Greek, Persian and Indian languages under the vigorous leadership of Harūn al-Rashīd and al-Ma'mūn. As a result of these translations the Muslim scholars were greatly influenced by foreign sciences particularly Greek science and philosophy. The works of Plato and Aristotle were regarded as important as the Qur'ān. Some of the Muslim philosophers interpreted the tenets of Islam in the light of Aristotelian philosophy and tried to harmonise the teachings of Islam with Greek philosophy. This led to springing up of many controversial philosophical doctrines like those of the Mu'tazila.[3] The Abbasid rulers particularly al-Mā'mūn patronised these doctrines and tried to impose them on the Muslims at the point of sword. This situation resulted in organized opposition by the orthodox Muslim religious scholars and theologians. The four great Muslim theologians *i.e.* Imām Abū Ḥanīfa (d. 767 A.D.), Imām Mālik (d. 795 A.D.), Imām Shafi'ī (d. 825 A.D.) and Imām Aḥmad bin Ḥanbal (d. 855 A.D.) lived in this period but they did not toe the line of the caliphs on religious matters.

Education, during this period was on the same lines as in earlier periods *i.e.* the Qur'ān formed the basis of education. The boys were taught reading, writing, grammar, philology, morals and offering of prayers. Of this lot the Qur'ān and the rituals were obligatory while the rest were voluntary. It will be of interest to quote the directive of Hārūn al-Rashīd to the teacher of al-Mā'mūn : "Teach him the Qur'ān, acquaint him with history, let him recite poetry, instruct him in *Sunnah*, give him skill in conversation. Do not make him unhappy for this will kill his comprehension but do not be too lenient to him"[4]. This quotation shows that education of the princes was somewhat different from the education imparted to the children of the common people. The elementary education was followed by advanced courses in the Qur'ān, Ḥadīth, Arabic language and literature and philosophy etc. These courses were conducted by learned scholars in mosques. Imām Shafi'ī held classes on Quranic exegesis, traditions, philosophy, rhetoric, grammar and poetry.[5] Al-Ṭabarī taught poetry in the mosque of Amar.[6] Al-Jubaī a noted Mu'tazilite (ninth century) lectured on philosophy in a mosque in Baṣra.[7] In addition to mosques there were other places for teaching and research such as Bait al-Ḥikma, Dar al-'Ilm and libraries. Bait al Ḥikma was founded by al-Mā'mūn[8] (833 A.D.) which consisted of a library, translation bureau, observatory and dormitaries for scholars. Khizānat al-Ḥikma was founded by Yaḥya[9] and Dar al-'Ilm by Ja'far bin Muḥammad in al-Mauṣīl.[10] During this period some Madrasas were also to be found where instruction was imparted in religion and philosophy such as the one founded by al-Baihaqī at Nisabūr.[11]

(iv) *Education under later Abbasids and during the disintegration of the Empire* : *The Buwehids* : After the death of Wāthiq the weakening of Abbasid power began. In 'Irāq the Buwehids became so powerful that they made and unmade the caliphs. They professed Shiism and supported scholars who expounded Shia doctrines. Their education system gave prominent place to elucidation of Shia doctrines. Aḍud al-daula founded a library called Khizanat al-Kutub in Shirāz. The Buwehids patronised philosophers and scholars. Al-Fārābī was associated with the Buwehid court.

The Seljūqs : In 1055 A.D. Tughral Beg the Seljūq made himself the master of 'Irāq. He helped the Abbasid calips in subjugating the Buwehids but in turn made them subservient to himself. He also checked the power of the Fatimids of

Egypt. Malik Shāh one of the Seljūq rulers was the most illustrious ruler of the dynasty. Niẓāmul Mulk was his talented minister who established Madrasas for the promotion of Islamic learning. The institutions attracted scholars from all parts of the Islamic world. Some people think that Niẓāmul Mulk was the founder of the institution of Madrasa but it was not so as some Madrasas existed before him as pointed out earlier.[12] Niẓāmul-Mulk only re-organised and reformed higher religious education by establishing some Madrasas as models for imparting higher religious education. These Madrasas were located in important towns of the empire such as Baghdad, Nīsābūr, Herāt, and al-Mauṣil. One of the close associates of Niẓāmul Mulk was al-Ghazzālī who formulated the new system of Islamic education by reviving purely Islamic sciences and curbing the heretical ideas of Muslim philosophers, the Mu'tazila and the Faṭimids. Niẓāmul Mulk and al-Ghazzālī promoted sunnī doctrines. Al-Ghazzālī himself served as teacher in the Madrasas of Baghdad and Nīsābūr.

The Samanids : The Samanids of BuKhāra also patronised sciences and men of letters. Ibn Sīna and al-Birūnī lived in their court.

The Ghaznawids : Sultān Mahmūd was the most illustrious patron of sciences. He founded a Madrasa at Ghaznī to which a library was also attached. The Madrasa attracted students from all over Central Asia and Persia. Many great scholars flocked to his court such as al-Biruni, Ibn Sīna and Firdausī.

The Faṭimids : In Egypt in the tenth century A.D. the Faṭimids ruled. They professed Ismāī'lī faith. They believed that Muḥammad bin Isma'īl was the last and the greatest prophet. They attributed Divinity to Ḥazrat 'Alī and at the same time adopted some heretical views of the Greek philosophers. Politically their aim was to destroy the Abbasid caliphate and create doubts in the minds of the Muslims about the traditional concept of their religion so that they may accept the superiority of the Isma'īlī faith. All these activities were carried on in the name of prophet's family. So a large number of Muslims were attracted towards them. The Faṭimid rulers patronised sciences as well. They founded the Dār al-'Ilm or Dār al-Ḥikmah aṭ Cairo to teach and expound the doctrines of Shiism particularly those of the Ismailians.

(v) *Education in Spain* : The Arabs of Spain were the torch bearers of culture, civilisation and education between the middle of the eighth century and the end of the thirteenth. It was through them that the ancient and the Islamic sciences were transmitted to Europe. The Umayyad ruler al-Ḥakkam patronised learning and granted munificient bounties to scholars.[13] He founded the University of Cordova in the principal mosque of Abdur Reḥamn III, which rose to the position of great eminence among the educational institutions in the Islamic world. This university preceded both the Al-Azhar of Cairo and the Nizamia of Baghdad and attracted students not only from Spain but from other parts of Europe, Africa and Asia. Among the professors of this university were Ibn Qutaiba, the grammarian and Abu Ali Qalī the philologist.[14] The university had a library with a collection of about four lac books. The university included among its departments the disciplines of Astronomy, Mathematics, Medicine, Theology and Law. The enrolment ran into thousands. There were universities at Seville, Malaqa and Granada also. The courses in these universities comprised Theology, Jurisprudence, Medicine, Chemistry, Philosophy and Astronomy.[15] An inscription on the portals of the last named university read : "The world is supported by four things : the learning of the wise, justice of the great, the prayer of the righteous and valour of the brave".[16]

Primary education in Spain was based as in all Muslim countries on the reading and writing of the Qur'ān, Arabic language and grammar. Spain was the only country in the Islamic world where the percentage of literary was the highest. The teacher was held in greater esteem than his counterpart in the east. Women were also given facilities for education.

Education in India : By the tenth century A.D. India became famous as an important Islamic country to which Muslims thronged from all parts of the Islamic world, particularly because of the unstable conditions prevailing in most of the Islamic countries. There was one way traffic to India from the north-west. The marchers included businessmen, common people, scholars, sūfīs and saints. Thus in a short time there was a sizeable population of Muslims in the remotest corners of the new Islamic empire. Hence the need of imparting education to the younger generation of the Muslims. The education was of course on the same pattern as imparted in other Islamic countries *i.e.* religious education. Religious education had been in vogue in India ever since the Muslims came to India in about eighth century A.D. in Sindh. Thus the first institution of Islamic learning were to be found in cities like Daibal, Manṣūra and Multan, where the Qur'ān and Ḥadīth were taught in mosques. In northern India with the conquest of Punjab by Mahmūd of Ghazna Muslims spread in this region also. The result was that Lahore became the cultural centre for scholars, preachers, mystics coming from Iran and central Asia. After Maḥmūd Mohammad Ghori was one of the most important rulers who played a vital role in sowing the seed of education in India. He in spite of his political pre-occupations contributed to the cause of education and established some schools in Ajmere. He sent scholars to other parts of the country for imparting instruction in Islamic sciences. The founder of the slave dynasty, Qutubuddin Aibak who loved learned people established mosque schools in his provinces where religious education was imparted to the masses. Altutmish who was himself a scholar devoted maximum possible time for the encouragement of learned people.

The centres of learning were established during the Muslim rule throughout the country and Islamic law gradually spread with the expansion of Muslim empire in the Indian sub-continent. The Muizzi College at Delhi was one of the best centres of learning in the reign of Sultan Razia Begum. Nasiruddin was also a great scholar and he appreciated and rewarded scholarship.

The Khaljis gave a new shape to the educational system. Their period was highly favourable to the cultivation of literary knowledge in India. It was in fact during the Khalji regime that seeds of scholarship were properly nurtured and a rich harvest reaped. Jalaluddin, the first king of the dynasty was a great lover of learning. He invited scholars to his court. It was in this period that Amir Khusrau emerged as a great scholar and poet. He was also Incharge of the Imperial Library. The Sultan held him in high esteem and conferred upon him the honour of wearing white robes which the member of Imperial House and the nobles of the highest order alone could wear. Sultan Ghiasuddin Khalji established a Madrasa exclusively for women because he considered their education essential for the progress of the country.

The Tughlaq dynasty also encouraged education and scholarship. Mohammad bin Tughlaq was the most learned among the rulers of the period. He was thoroughly at home in almost all the subjects of Arts and Science. His literary interest attracted intellectual luminaries from far and wide. Firoz Shah Tughlaq was a brilliant student of History. He himself wrote an account of his reign. He respected the learned. Education during the reign of Firoz Shah Tughlaq made remarkable advance and education was for the first time organised on regular basis. He himself being an eminent educationist deputed teachers to various parts of the empire for the sake of imparting instruction to the people. This step brought far reaching reforms in the education system and produced a large number of scholars. He repaired and reconstructed old Madrasas which were in decaydent condition. He also established new schools and colleges with residential accommodation and paid handsome remuneration to the teachers. Some of the colleges attracted teachers from foreign countries. Education was an important item of state expenditure.

The Lodi dynasty also made valuable contribution to the educational policy and made improvements in the then existing system of education. He valued the society of learned men and loved the learned. He considered the promotion of education as his duty. The mission was further carried forward by sultan Sikandar Lodi who was a poet of distinction. Education made much progress in his reign and it was for the first time that education was made compulsory for the military officers. He gave fresh impulse to the art of writing, compilation and translation When he shifted his capital from Delhi to Agra he established centres of learning in the new capital. Agra became a radiant centre of Islamic culture and civilisation. Scholars from Arabia, Bukhara and Persia poured into Agra in ever increasing numbers. Soon Agra grew into a great centre of learning having several schools and colleges where people came for study from far flung areas. Education was also given due consideration in provincial kingdoms. All these Muslim rulers patronised Islamic education. The courses of studies were identical to that of 'Irāq, Syria, Spain and Khurāsān. Primary school were located in mosques where children learnt the Qur'ān. The syllabi of the institutions of higher learning included Arabic language and literature, Persian, Qur'ān, Ḥadīth, Fiqh, al-Kalām, Logic, Astronomy and Mathematics. In this period natural sciences and various schools of philosophy were not included in the syllabi but later on under the Mughals these subjects and many more secular subjects were added. (As the Mughal period is outside the scope of this study *i.e.* 14th to 17th century the development of Muslim education during the Mughal and the modern period has been traced in the Appendix.

References

1. Hameedullah : Education system in time of the Prophet Art. in *Islamic Culture* 13 (1939), pp. 48-59.
2. Nicholson : *Literary History of the Arabs*, pp. 193, 197.
3. The term 'Mu'tazilla' is derived from Itizal' (*i e.* to secede). The term originated in the course of a lecture delivered by Ḥasan al-Baṣrī (early 8th century) when one of his pupils differed from the views of learned lecturer and left the class and sat in another corner of the mosque. At this Ḥasan Baṣrī said 'I'tazala ana' (he seceded from us). This man was Wasil bin 'Aṭa. His followers were called Mu'tazila. Some leading Mutazalites were Huḍail Allāf. Al-Nazzam al-Jāhiz, al-Jubaī. The Mutazilites held different views from the commonly held views of the Muslims on freedom of man, the creation of the Qur'ān and the qualities of God as separate from Him etc.
4. Al-Masūdī : *Murūj al-dhahab* Vol. II, p. 194 also quoted by Ibn Khaldūn : *Muqaddima*, p. 306.
5. al-Tibawi : Muslim Education in the Golden Age of Caliphate. Art. in *Islamic Culture*, 28, 1954 . p. 433.
6. *Ibid.*
7. *Ibid.*

8. Pederson: Some Aspects of the History of Madrasa Art. in *Islamic Culture* 3, 1929 p. 529.
9. *Ibid.*, p. 530.
10. *Ibid.*
11. *Ibid.*
12. Al-Tibawi : Muslim Education in Golden Age of Islam Art. in *Islamic Culture*, 28, 1954, p. 436.
13. Hitti : *History of the Arabs*, p. 530.
14. *Ibid.*, p. 531.
15. *Ibid.*, p. 563.
16. *Ibid.*

Chapter II

PHILOSOPHICAL AND ETHICAL CONCEPTS OF THE QUR'ĀN INFLUENCING MUSLIM EDUCATIONAL THOUGHT

The Holy Qur'ān itself has determined the alpha and omega of Islamic education. The Qur'ān contains many verses which speak of the philosophical subjects such as 'Ultimate Reality', 'Knowledge', 'Freedom and Authority', 'Life after death' etc. These concepts alluded to in the Qur'ān served as the point of reference for the philosophers of Islam who studied Greek philosophy and tried to bring about an accord between philosophy and tenets of Islam. Some of the philosophers faltered no doubt but in their effort at reconciliation lies the enrichment of Islamic philosophy and the Islamic education system.

Some philosophical concepts of the Qur'ān

Ultimate Reality : "The ultimate Being or the Reality is God".[1]

"God is one and there is no God but He".[2]

"God is omnipotent, to Him is due the primate origin of everything".[3]

"He is the creator".[4]

"He created the Heavens and the earth".[5]

"He is the sole self subsisting, all pervading, Absolute Reality".[6]

"He created the sun, the moon and the stars, all governed by laws ordained by Him and under His command".[7]

"Every creature in Heavens and earth submits to His laws".[8]

Freedom of the Will

"God has given man the will to choose, to decide and resolve to do good or evil. He has endowed him with reason and various impulses so that by his own effort he may strive and explore" (18 : 29).

Life after death : "God created man from the earth into it he shall return and from it he will be brought out again. For every one after death there will be an interval lasting till the day of judgment".[9]

The Source of Knowledge : "Truth comes from God alone, so be not of those who doubt".[10]

"God is all knowledge. He is truth, with him are the keys of the unseen, the treasures that none knows but He".

Kinds of Knowledge : "There are three degrees of knowledge : "Knowledge by inference", "Knowledge by perception", "Knowledge by intuition".[11]

"Man has been given knowledge which angels do not possess".[12]

"Knowledge of the phenomenal world is not an illusion but a blessing for which man must be thankful".[13]

Benefits of Knowledge : "Whoever is given knowledge has indeed been given abundant good".[14]

"Only those people will be given higher ranks who have faith and who possess knowledge".[15]

"Can those who possess knowledge and those who do not possess knowledge be on equal footing".[16]

"O my Lord, Increase me in knowledge".[17]

Incidentally it may be pointed out that Prophet Mohammad (Peace be on him) pointed out the importance of knowledge which is evident from these well known traditions :

"He dies not who seeks knowledge".

"Seeking of knowledge is obligatory for every Muslim, man and woman".

"Seek knowledge even though in China".

"He who leaves his home in search of knowledge walks in the path of Allah".

"A word of wisdom is like the lost treasure of a believer who has got the best right to secure it wherever he might find it".

"An hour's contemplation and study of God's creation is better than a year of adoration".

"Acquire knowledge. He who acquired it in the way of Allah performs an act of piety; he who speaks of it praises the Lord; he who seek adores God; he who dispenses instruction in it bestows alms; he who imparts it to the deserving person performs an act of devotion".

"A father can confer on his children nothing more valuable than the gift of education; it is better that a man should secure a good education for his children than he should leave a treasure of gold and silver".

Qur'ān on Cultivation of Science

"He taught Adam the nature of all things".[18]

"God has ordained every thing in the skies and the earth for your service. In this there are signs for the thoughtful".[19]

"Proclaim. And thy Lord is most bountiful. He taught man the use of pen which he knew not".[20]

"Those truly fear God among his servants who have knowledge".[21]

"He it is who made the sun a shining brightness and the moon a light and ordained for it mansions that you might know the computation of years and reckon. God has created these with a purpose. He explains his signs to those who (want to) know".[22]

Worship of God : According to Qur'ān the core of human existence is worship of God. Here are the words of the Qu'rān :

"I have created the Jinn and men only that they may worship Me."[23]

"Say verily, my prayers, my sacrifice, my life, my death are all for Allāh, the Lord of the Worlds. He has no peer".[24]

Thus we can say that the Islamic system of education comprised of two elements :

1. The basic elements based on the Qur'ān and Ḥadīth which cannot be changed.

2. The non-basic element which can be changed according to the needs of the time. The basic elements included belief in

God and his prophet Moḥammad (Peace be on him) and the way of life enjoined by the Qur'ān and Prophet. The non-basic element included foreign sciences such as philosophy, mathematics, astronomy etc.

Religious and social virtues : The Qur'ān specially emphasise the inculcation of virtues like patience, repentence, fear of God, truthfulness, righteousness etc. The Qur'ān says :

"O ye who believe seek help with patience and with prayer, for God is with the patient" (2 : 148).

"But whoever shall repent to God after his wickedness and amend, God truly will turn to him, for God is oft forgiving, merciful".[25]

"Be thankful to God for whoever is thankful is thankful for his own soul and if any shall be ungrateful God truly is self sufficient and worthy of all praise".[26]

"Righteousness consists of believing in one and only one God, and the last Day; and the Angels and the Books and the Massengers; and to spend in God's way out of your wealth that you love, for your kith and kin, for orphans, for the needy, for the wayfarer and for ransom of slaves and to keep up prayer and to practice charity and to fulfil the contracts which you have made and to forbearing hardship and adversity and in time of distress. Such are the people who love truth, such are the people who fear God".[27]

Some social values specifically emphasised in Ḥadīth are as follows :

"The Muslim should not wish unto Muslim brother what he does not wish to be done unto himself".

"A Muslim brother should not be hurt by an unkind word or an unbecoming deed".

"If one is angry with a Muslim he should not prolong his anger for more than three days".

"One should be good to all and repay evil with good".

"One should not disclose the defects and secrets of other Muslims".

Condemnation of social vices : Islam condemned the generally prevalent vices such as pride, slandering, back biting and love of wealth etc.

The Qur'ān says :

"And walk not proudly on earth. Verily God does not like the proud".[28]

"Woe to every slanderer, backbiter who piles up wealth and goes on counting and recounting, thinking that his wealth could be with him for ever".[29]

Islamic concept of the nature of Man

Man has a dual nature, he is both soul and body. Man has been given knowledge about God His absolute oneness and the necessity of worshipping Him. God is the true Lord and true object of worship.[30] (see quotations from Qur'ān pp. 11-12). The seat of this knowledge is the spirit or soul of man (*i.e.* heart) and the intellect. Thus belief in God and worshipping Him is part and parcel of man's nature. To guide man to the right path God has equipped him with faculty of right vision provided an effort is made by him. This will help him in discrimination of right from wrong and truth from falsehood. Further it is necessary that man should try to assert the supremacy of the rational soul and suppress the animal soul. If man achieves this the truth will dawn upon him and he will obey the command of God.

Islamic concept of knowledge : According to Qur'ān God is the source of all knowledge and He has given knowledge to man (see quotations from the Qur'ān p. 12-13). Some of the knowledge is revealed by God to the Prophet Moḥammad (Peace be on him) through the Qur'ān which comprises essentials of morals and faith etc. and some knowledge is given to man through his own effort. This includes knowledge related to the natural phenomena.

Classification of knowledge according to Muslim Philosophers

According to Ibn Bajja human knowledge is of two kinds :

1. Knowledge based on proof 2. Knowledge based on direct experience through religious devotion and revelation. The knowledge obtained by the sufis is obtained by religious devotion while the knowledge of the prophet is revealed by God.

Al-Fārābī has classified knowledge into practical and

theoretical. The latter knowledge help the soul to achieve perfection and the former is related to conduct.

According to al Ghazzālī There are two types of knowledge *viz.* the intuitive knowledge and the knowledge acquired by rational effort. The intuitive knowledge leads to perfection of the soul and the knowledge acquired through experience, observation and rational effort leads to development of sciences.

FaKhruddīn Rāzī classifies and defines various Muslim sciences in his book *Jami'al-Ulūm.* Among the religious sciences he mentions theology, jurisprudence, dialectics, Qur'ān and Ḥadīth. Then he deals the linguistic sciences such as grammar, syntax, etymology, prosody and poetry. He calls these sciences Naqlī or traditional sciences. The other branch of knowledge are the 'Aqlī (based on intellect); these sciences include natural philosophy, physics, astronomy, alchamy, optics and music.

Ibn Khaldūn classifies knowledge into two kinds *viz.* 'Ulūm Ṭabai'yya or 'Aqlīyya and 'Ulūm Naqliyya. The former are based observation and deduction and the later depend on revelation. 'Ulūm 'Aqliyya comprise Logic, Arithmetic, Astronomy, Physical and Biological Sciences etc. and 'Ulūm Naqliyya include Qur'ān, Ḥadīth, Fiqh, Kalām, Theology etc.

Noblest knowledge according to Islam : The knowledge given by God through revelation *i.e.* the Qur'ān is the noblest of knowledge. The Qur'ān is complete and final revelation from God so it is a complete guide for man in worldly affairs as well as for his salvation. Hence there is no other knowledge except that which is based on the Qur'ān that can guide man. The Qur'ān is the knowledge *par excellenee.* The life and teachings of prophet Moḥammad (Peace be on him) on whom the Qur'ān was revealed is the most perfect interpretation of the Qur'ān. So the prophet's life and sayings (Ḥadīth) are true guide for Muslims. So, the Qur'ān, the Ḥadīth, the Shariyah (God's Laws) are the essential elements of knowledge worth acquiring for a Muslim. Devotion to God through worship is the practical aspect of the knowledge acquired through the Qur'ān and the Ḥadīth.

The second kind of knowledge which is knowledge of sciences should also be acquired by the Muslims. However, the first find of knowledge which reveals the true relationship between man and God should form the basis and foundation for the second. If the knowledge of the second kind is obtained without reference to the first then it will lead to confusion and will create doubt and skepticism. It is because of this fact that Muslim philosophers made the knowledge based on the Qur'ān and Ḥadīth obligatory for all Muslims and the knowledge of Sciences obligatory for some people who can do justice to it.

References

1. *Holy Qur'ān* (2 : 186).
2. *Ibid.*, (2 : 163).
3. *Ibid.*, (10 : 4).
4. *Ibid.*, (96 : 1).
5. *Ibid.*, (10 : 2).
6. *Ibid.*, (2 : 115).
7. *Ibid.*, (7 : 54).
8. *Ibid.*, (3 : 85).
9. *Ibid.*, (20 : 55).
10. *Ibid.*, (3 : 60).
11. *Ibid.*, (102 : 5), (102 : 7), (69 : 51).
12. *Ibid.*, (2 : 31).
13. *Ibid.*, (16 : 78).
14. *Ibid.*, (2 : 269).
15. *Ibid.*, (58 : 11).
16. *Ibid.*, (39 : 9).
17. *Ibid.*, (20 : 114).
18. *Ibid.*, (2 : 31).
19. *Ibid.*, (45 : 13).
20. *Ibid.*, (96 : 3-5).
21. *Ibid.*, (35 : 28).
22. *Ibid.*, (10 : 5).
23. *Ibid.*, (51 : 56).
24. *Ibid.*, (6 : 162).
25. *Ibid.*, (5 : 43).

26. *Ibid.*, (31 : 11).
27. *Ibid*,, (2 : 177).
28. *Ibid.*, (31 : 18).
29. *Ibid.*, (104 : 1-4).
30. *Ibid.*

CHAPTER III

IDEAS AND IDEOLOGIES INFLUENCING MUSLIM EDUCATIONAL THOUGHT

In the lands of Islam flowed many streams of knowledge such as philosophy, theology and Sufism all of which influenced Muslim Educational Thought. We begin by tracing the influence of philosophy.

A. *Philosophy*

The philosophical ideas of the Muslims were greatly influenced by Greek Philosophy as well as the philosophical concepts of the Qur'ān (which are discussed in detail in the preceding Chapter). The Greek philosophy and the effort of the Muslim philosophers for harmonising it with the philosophical concepts of the Qur'ān dates back to the translation of Greek works which began in the Umayyad period and reached the climax under al-Ma'mūn. Among the Greek philosophers who wielded great influence on Muslim philosophers were Plato, Aristotle and the neo-Platonists like Plotinus etc. It is, therefore, worthwhile to delineate some of the basic concepts of these philosophers followed by the philosophical concepts of the Muslim philosphers.

Plato

Plato's concept of knowledge : Knowledge according to Plato was the grasping of the true meaning of a thing. True nature of a thing according to Plato cannot be known through sense perception. True being of a thing is its idea, its eternally unchangeable and universal nature. It can be known by special method of enquiry. The method employed by him was the dialectic method of Socrates. He developed the theory of this method in order to discover with the help of reason the true nature of the universal idea.

Cosmology : Plato believed that God the maker of the world fashioned human body out of four elements gifted with soul as well as intelligence.

Soul : The soul[1] according to Plato is immaterial and prior to body. It is gifted with power to know the ultimate truth. The body is intended by nature to be its servant and to listen to its commands. Once the soul lived with God in the world of ideas. On release from body it has to give an account of itself before God. Those who have been virtuous in this world are sent after earth to the Isle of the Blessed and the wicked to Tartarus to suffer punishment.

Ethics : According to Plato the highest good of life is harmony of the soul which is attained by the exercise of wisdom, courage, temperance and justice under the guidance of reason.[2] The greatest happiness attends the life that achieves the highest good and contemplates the highest ideas.

Aristotle

He was a pupil of Plato but his philosophical ideas were in some cases diametrically opposed to those of his master's. Aristotle wrote on many subjects. The collection of his work on logic is entitled *Organon*, his other writings are *Metaphysica*, *Rhetorica* and *Poetica*.

Aristotle's Metaphysics : Aristotle believed that the essence or form of things exists only in those things, they are immanent in them. The world of sensible things is therefore the real world.[3] In this concept he differed from Plato who thought that the form exists in the world of ideas.

Ethics : According to Aristotle the ultimate end of man is happiness. Human excellence expresses itself in virtue. By virtue he meant the habitual direction of the will to follow the golden mean.[4] For example the virtue of courage is the mean between cowardice and dare devilness. Human happiness manifests itself in two ways, first, in habitual subordination of the animal side of man's nature, his appetites, desires and passions to rational rule. Second, in the exercise of reason in search of knowledge and contemplation of Truth. Thus happiness expresses itself in moral virtues like courage, temperance, magnanimity and justice. In short Aristotle was a rationalist while Plato was an idealist.

Neo-Platonists : *Plotinus* : He was conversant with the principal doctrines of all the philosophical schools of the Greeks particularly those of Plato and Aristotle. The purpose of philosophy according to him was cosmic as well as religious. His work is entitled the *Enneads*.

Perphyry : He wrote a commentary on Plato in which he tried to show that Plato was mystic.

Greek influence on Muslim Philosophers : The influence of Greek philosophy on Muslim philosophers may be traced back to translations of Greek works by Muslim Savants like Ḥunain bin Ishāq. Qustā bin Lūqa, T̲h̲ābit bin Qurrā etc. besides the Muslim philosophers themselves translated the philosophical works of Greek masters from original sources. However, it may be pointed out that some of the translations and commentaries which gained currency among the Muslim philosophers were incorrect. Their interpreters gave religious and mystical colour to their philosophy and they confused them with neo-Platonic philosophers, so they attributed neo-Platonic ideas to Plato and Aristotle. A Christian named Nayemah of Emessa translated the last three books of *Enneads* of Plotinus into Arabic and named it as *Theology of Aristotle*.[5] In this book he proved that human soul cannot know God through reason. God could be known through ecstasy. It is therefore not surprising that Muslim philosophers tried to harmonise the teaching of Plato and Aristotle with the tenets of Islam. It was only al-G̲h̲azzālī who depricated this tendency of the Muslim philosophers because this according to him sowed the seeds of heresy and skepticism.

Muslim Philosophers

Al-Kindī (801-870 A.D.). Al-Kindī flourished under al-Mā'mūn and al-Mu'taṣim. He was the first Arab scholar who mastered the philosophy of Aristotle and Plato and tried to harmonise Greek philosophy with the tenets of Islam. He is known as the 'Philosopher of the Arabs.'[6] He borrowed from

Plotinus the doctrine of soul and followed Aristotle in his theory of intellect. He relied on reason as source of truth and at the same time believed that revelation also guided humanity to the same goal. However, it was because of his rationalistic ideas that he was persecuted during orthodox reaction under al-Mutawakkil.

Al-Fārābī (870-950. A.D.). Al-Fārābī was another great philosopher of Islam. His philosophy was a syncretic of Platonism, Aristotelianism and Sufism.[7] He understood and interpreted Aristotle's Logic so perfectly and unravelled the mystries of Greek philosophy so comprehensively that he was called the 'second teacher', the first being Aristotle. Besides his knowledge of the philosophy and logic of Aristotle from original sources he was also influenced by the so called *Theology of Aristotle*, a late neo-Platonic writing (*supra* p. 21) This factor helped him to bring an accord between Aristotelian philosophy and the tenets of Islam. However, al-Fārābī sometimes gave a rational interpretation of religious truth and hence he alienated the orthodox theologians.

Ibn Sīna (980-1037 A.D.) : He was also a great philosopher of the period who built an elaborate and complete system of philosophy based on Aristotle with a tinge of neo-Platonism.[8] He also aimed at harmonisation of Greek philosophy with Islam However he could not conceal his rational outlook in his concept of the eternity, the doctrine of prophethood and resurrection of body. In the lands of Islam his philosophy dominated for about a century after the death but declined as a result of the criticism of al-Ghazzālī. However, in Europe he was greatly admired for his philosophical ideas for many centuries.

Ibn Miskawaih (932-1030 A.D.) : Ibn Miskawaih was a contemporary of Ibn Sīna. He discussed the tenets of Islam philosophically such as the existence and unity of God, the nature of prophesy and happiness of soul etc. However, his fame rests on his contribution to Islamic ethics which is discussed in his book *Tahdhīb al Akhlaq*. One chapter of this book is devoted to education of youth and children. (For his theory of education see chapter IV).

Al-Ghazzālī (1058-1111 A.D.) : Al-Ghazzālī was a great

scholar of Islam. His studies covered an extensive range of subjects particularly theology, fiqh, science, philosophy, mysticism etc. His fame rests as the defender of Islamic metaphysical concepts against the onslaught of the philosophers and other rationalists who propagated un-Islamic beliefs and notions under the garb of rationalism. He wrote a book on the refutation of the philosophers who were dubbed as heretics and un-Islamic. He tried to prove Islamic metaphysical concepts by means of arguments. The sciences of argument was called 'Ilm al-Kalām.

Ibn Rushd (1126-1198 A.D.) : Ibn Rushd was of Spanish origin. He was a philosopher in the tradition of Ibn Sīna and Al-Fārābī. He started by writing commentaries on the books of Aristotle and later wrote independent works on philosophy. In his works he defended philosophy against the attack of theologians in general and al-Ghazzālī in particular. Like other Muslim philosopher his aim was to bring about an accord between Islam and philosophy. Ibn-Rushd, however, could not make a dent in the Islamic world in which al-Ghazzālī continued to be regarded as the 'Argument of Islam'. Ibn Rushd was better known and appreciated in medieval Europe through Latin translations of his works, as Europe was interested in the scientific and rationalist approach presented by Ibn-Rushd.

B. Philosophical Schools

The Mo'tazila : This school of thought arose towards the middle of the eighth century. It stood for the rational interpretation of faith and religious beliefs. Allāf and Nazzam were two eminent exponents of the Mo'tazilite school who were al-Mā'mūn's teachers. Al-Jāhiz was another philosopher who subscribed to the views of the Mo'tazila. The Mo'tazilites held many views which were against the tenets of Islam such as the view that the powers of God were limited, that man has power over his action so he should not be punished for his actions in the world hereafter, that the qualities of God are separate entities from Him, similarly they held beliefs on many other fundamental matters contrary to the traditional views of the theologians. They gave rational interpretation of these questions. The Mo'tazilites thrived under the patronage of early Abassids caliphs but al-Mutawakkil suppressed them. Thus their influence declined in the heart land of Islam but still their influence continued for some time longer under the Fatimids and the Buwehids.

The Ikhwān al-Ṣafā: This was a secret society of philosophers and thinkers of radical ideas. They lived at a time (Mid Tenth century A.D.) when free thought was persecuted so they kept their deliberations secret and compiled the then existing Greek knowledge into a volume comprising 52 tracts. They came into open after the Buwehids captured Baghdad and preached heretical doctrines in name of free thought. Their system was eclectic comprising the ideas of Plato, Aristotle, Mō'tazila and the Ismā'ilīs. Their ideas were totally unacceptable to the orthdox Muslims.

Al-Ashā'rism (Tenth Century A.D.): This was a philosophic-religious school of thought in Islam. This movement was an attempt to purge Islam of all non-Islamic elements which were introduced into Islam in the name of rationalism. The leader of the Movement was Abul Ḥasan 'Alī b. Ismā'il al-Ash'arī (.945 A.D.). His movement was a reaction against the Mo'tazila on the one hand and the orthodox theologians, traditionalists, jurists etc. on the other who adhered to the literal interpretation of the Qur'ān and the sunnah and pleaded for blind faith in every dogma. In order to fight these forces he laid the foundation of orthodox Kalām as opposed to the rationalist Kalām of the Mu'tazilites and the philosophers. With the help of this science of Kalām he proved Islamic concepts by reasoning and arguments and defended Islam against the attacks of the philosophers and the Mo'tazilites. The movement was strengthened by the efforts of al-Ghazzālī who himself was not an Ash'arite but who wrote a book on the refutation of Muslim philosophers and the rationalists. He also paid attention to reorganisation of education system so as to purge it of un-Islamic views.

C. *Theology*

The theologians codified and systematised social and religious laws in the form of jurisprudence in the light of

Ḥadīt͟h and the Qur'ān. Imām S͟hafi'ī was the first to lay down the rules of jurisprudence. In addition to him there were three more renowned Imams of jurisprudence *viz.* Imām Abū Ḥanīfa, Imām Mālik and Imām Aḥmad bin Ḥambal. The great traditionists (scholars of Ḥadīt͟h) were Imām Buk͟hārī, Imām Muslim, Tirmid͟hi and Nas'aī. These theologians believed in the words of the Qur'ān and Ḥadīt͟h literally. They did not allow any discussion concerning matters clearly given in the Qur'ān and the Ḥadīt͟h.

A parallel school of theology was founded by the S͟hi'a sect. The S͟hia's believed in the divine right of the prophet's family to wield supreme authority in Islam both temporal and spiritual. The S͟hi'as upheld the claim of Ḥaḍrat 'Alī as the real successor of the prophet. They further believed that the descendants of Ḥaḍrat 'Alī were the real divinely appointed Imāms of the Muslims. Thus they questioned the legality of bestowing temporal and spiritual leadership of the Muslims to Ḥaḍrat Abū Bakr, followed by Ḥaḍrat 'Omar, Ḥaḍrat 'Ut͟hmān and lastly Ḥaḍrat 'Ali, as accepted by the mainstreams of the Muslims. The matter was further aggravated by the grabbing of the power by Umayyads. The tragedy of Karbala added fuel to the fire. Thus the differences between the S͟hi'as and other Muslims had two aspects—one was the question of Imāmat and the other was political. The S͟hi'as wanted to dislodge the Umayyads from the caliphate. The Persians who were run over by the second caliph Haḍrat 'Umar and who were treated by the Umayyads with contempt took up the cause of the S͟hi'ās. As regards spiritual matters as already pointed out the Shias believed in divinely appointed Imams. The first three being Ḥaḍrat 'Alī, Imām Ḥasan and Imām Ḥusain. His step brother Ibn Ḥanafiyya was accepted as the next Imām. After his death two different groups were formed, one group regarded Abū Hāshim the son of Muḥammad bin Ḥanafiyya as the Imām while the other group elevated 'Alī, son of Ḥusain known as Zainul 'Abidīn as the Imām. The first group was called Hashimiyya and the other Imamiyya. The sixth Imām was J'afer al-Ṣādiq. However, as a result of his disqualifying his eldest son Isma'īl and nominating his younger son Müsa al-Kāzim for Imamat two factions arose. They followers of

Mūsa and his five successors were called Ithna 'Asharī and the followers of Ismā'il were known as Ismāi'li's. These Imams codified the social and religious laws for their followers.

D. *Ṣūfism*

Ṣūfism started as a reaction against the formalism of the theologians and the intellectualism of the rationalists. The Ṣūfīs were against life of pomp and luxury as lived by the caliphs and other dignitories and they shunned their company. They lived a life of austerity on the lines of the prophet Muḥammad (Peace be on him), and the Pious Caliphs. The name of Ṣūfī was given to them.

There are various views about the origin of the word Ṣūfī.[9] Some people think that it was derived from al-Ṣafa (purity) or from al-Saffāh (an elevated corner in the courtyard of Masjid Nabawī) or from al-Ṣaf (row). All these views are improbable from the point of view of linguistic analogy. The same applies to its derivation from al-Ṣūf (wool) because the Ṣūfīs were not the only people who wore wool. Ibn Khaldūn was of the view that the latter view was correct because the Ṣūfīs as a rule were characterised by wearing woollen garments and were opposed to people wearing gorgeous dress and therefore chose to wear course cloth made of wool.

As regards the influencing factor on Ṣūfī ideology there are different views. Some people think that Ṣūfī ideology was influenced by Persian and Greek ideas, some people think that they were influenced by the sophists of Greece. However, these views are not substantiated by reliable evidence. The truth seems to be that Sufism had a purly Islamic origin as its historical development shows.

Ṣūfīsm from its very inception came to represent retirement from the world of pomp and luxury and devotion to divine worship resulting in a particular kind of perception which comes about ecstatic experience. Ibn Khaldūn points out that three main stages of the development of Ṣūfīsm are discernible.[10] At the first stage they devoted their lives to prayers both incumbent and superarogatory. They retired from society and avoided every form of luxury. Ḥasan of

Başra (728 A.D.). Ibrāhim bin Adham (777 A.D.) and Rabi'ya Başrī (776 A.D.). belonged to this stage. At the second stage of development the doctrines of Şūfīsm began to take shape. Ma'rūf of Karkh (815 A.D.) formulated the doctrine of total forgetfulness. Sari Tagate (870 A.D.) initiated the doctrine of *tauhid* which became the central idea of Şūfī philosophy. Ibrahim Dhun Nūn Mişrī (859 A.D.) introduced the doctrine of *ḥal* (state) and *Maqām* (stage) and ecstacy. He wrote treatises wherein he expounded the mystical doctrines of Sufism. At the third stage the philosophy of pantheism was introduced according to which the distinction between the creator and the created is obliterated. Manşūr al-Hallāj betrays pantheistic tendencies in his utterance *Ana al-Ḥaq* (I am the Truth). It was at this stage that the breach between theology and Şūfīsm took place. The theologians held that the *Shari'at* (formal religious laws) are very important for the Muslims as against this the Şūfīs believed that *Ṭarīqat* (spirit of religion) is more important than form. The Şūfīs therefore followed *Ṭarīqat* for the salvation of the soul.

Some leading Şūfī scholars wrote laws governing asceticism and self scrutiny. Al-Muḥāsib was one such writer. The şūfī writers also wrote on the behaviour of the sufis and the different kinds of the mystical and ecstatic experiences, al-Qusharī and al-Suhrawardī did this job. Al-Ghazzālī who later in his life was greatly impressed by some of the doctrines of Şūfīsm made an attempt at the reconciliation of the views of the theologians and the Şūfīs. Attempts at reconciliation were also made by Junaid of Baghdad who held the view that *Shari'at* and *Tarīqat* are two aspects of Islam which are supplementary to each other.

All these diverse streams of knowledge converged on education. These schools of thought produced huge literature in their respective fields and produced great masters of their respective schools of thought, who were also great teachers of their times. In the beginning the teaching was done in the mosques but later on Madrasas were established where religious and philosophical subjects were taught such as the Qur'ān, Ḥadīth, theology, philosophy and Şūfīsm etc.

References

1. M.M. Sharif : *History of Muslim Philosophy*, Vol. I, p. 96.
2. *Ibid.*, p. 96.
3. *Ibid.*
4. *Ibid.*, p. 98.
5. Umaruddin : *Ethical Philosophy of al-Ghazzali*, Aligarh 1962. p. 27.
6. Sarton : *An Introduction to the History of Science*, Baltimore 1927. 1948 Vol. I, p. 559.
7. *Ibid.*, Vol. I, p. 628.
8. *Ibid.*, pp. 709-710.
9. Ibn Khaldūn : *Muqaddima* (English translation by Rosenthal), Vol. III, p. 76.
10. *Ibid.*

Chapter IV

EDUCATIONAL PHILOSOPHY OF IBN MISKAWAIH

Abu Aḥmad bin Moḥammad bin Ya'qūb surnamed Miskawaih[1] was born in al-Ray in 932 A.D. (died 1030 A.D.). His father was an employee of the rulers so he got an opportunity of mixing with the nobility and the officials. The learned society in which he moved created in him the desire for studies. As a young man he became attached to al-Muhallabī the vazier of the Buwehid prince Mu'izz al-daula in Baghdad. After al-Muhallabī's death he obtained the favour of Ibn al-Āmid the vazier of Mu'izz al-daula's brother Rukn al-daula at at al-Ray. Ibn Miskawaih served as librarian in Ibn al-Āmid's Library. Here he was able to pursue his studies. Afterwards he went to Baghdad and became attached to the court of Aḍud al-daula. Ibn Miskawaih took keen interest in history, philosophy and ethics. He wrote a number of books on these subjects. He was influenced by Plato, Aristotle, Galen, Perphery and the Stoics.

Philosophical concepts of Ibn Miskawaih : His philosophical ideas are to be found in his book *al-Fauz al-Aṣghar*. He has discussed his philosophical ideas in three parts. The first part deals with the proof of the existence of God. The second part deals with soul. The third part deals with prophethood. In this book Ibn Miskawaih has tried to reconcile Greek ideas with the tenets of Islam.

Ibn Miskawaih's Concept of Soul : According to him the soul is nobler and higher than the bodily things. Further, the soul longs for that which is not bodily. It is interested in knowing the reality of the divine and turns away from pleasure of body to seek those of intellect. He divides soul into three faculties : (i) The rational faculty which reflects and discerns realities of things. (ii) The concupiscent faculty which finds expression in desires for worldly things. (iii) The irascible faculty which finds expression in passion and anger. These three faculties are distinct from each other. The over-development of one impairs the others. He also says that the rational faculty is called kingly and the organ of the body which uses it is brain. The concupiscent faculty is called beastly and the organ of the body which uses it is liver. The irascible faculty is called the leonine and the organ of the body which uses it is the heart.

Morality and Ethics : Following Plato, he draws a parallel between the faculties of the soul and the corresponding virtues of wisdom, courage and temperance. By the harmony of these three virtues is produced the fourth virtue namely justice. The opposite of these virtues are called vices.

Ibn Miskawaih follows Aristotle in his concept of human happiness which is achieved by subordination of the animal side of man's nature, his appetites and desires to rational rule. This manifests itself in four cardinal virtues as propounded by Aristotle *viz.* courage, temperance, wisdom and justice. Ibn Miskawaih divided wisdom into seven kinds[4] such as acuteness of intelligence, quickness of intellect, clearness of understanding, facility of acquirement, precision of discrimination, retention and recollection. Similarly he divided courage in various kinds.[5]

Ibn Miskawaih's Concept of Knowledge

He discusses knowledge in the background of his concept of soul, which can achieve the knowledge of ultimate reality and possesses rational knowledge. Like Socrates he considers knowledge as the basis of good character and says the root of all virtue is knowledge so in the acquisition of knowledge lies human perfection. The various activities of the soul are directed to this end but the physical senses act as a veil between him and the goal. Man also possesses the faculty of volition which distinguishes good from bad. This faculty helps in removing the veil. But all rational beings cannot attain the knowledge of ultimate reality as they are born with different capacities. He further says that the power of the intellect has two aspects—the theoretical and the practical. The function of the practical faculty is the perfection of character and the improvement of conduct and the function of theoretical faculty is perfection of science.[7]

Ibn Miskawaih's concept of character[8]

Ibn Miskawaih defines character as a state of the soul which causes it to perform its action without thought or deliberation. This state is of two kinds. One is natural and originates in the temperament as in the man whom the least thing moves to anger or who is aroused from the least cause. The other kind is that which is acquired by habit and self training. It may have its beginning in deliberations and thought but then it becomes by gradual and continued practice an aptitude and trait of character.

Ibn Miskawaih quotes the views of ancient Greeks about character. He says : The Stoics believed that all men are created good by nature, they have become bad as a result of association to wicked passion that cannot be tamed by discipline. Galen on the other hand observes that some men are good by nature and others are bad by nature and still others fall between the two. The people who are good by nature are very few and cannot become bad, others who are bad by nature are numerous they do not become good. The group which falls between the two may become good by accompanying good people or turn bad by associating with bad people. Aristotle believed that a bad man by discipline may become good but he did not consider this to hold absolutely because some people are responsive to discipline but acquire it slowly.

Ibn Miskawaih on Character Training[10]

Character is not natural it is acquired. Changes in character can be brought about gradually. So men who want to attain purity of character should follow the natural way. For this it is necessary that the child can differentiate between good and bad and can think. Learning good habits depends on thinking and willing, this quality is produced at a particular stage in man's life. The child possess modesty so he does not want to do undesirable acts. He has also got self respect so also he avoids undesirable act. All these must be taken into consideration. People acquire good traits which we have called character because of their eagerness to learn and to care for them. If innate nature is neglected and not subjected to discipline or correction every man will grow up in accordance with his own nature and will remain all his life in the condition in which he was in childhood.

It is the law which reforms the young, accustoms them to good deeds, prepares their soul to receive wisdom, seek virtue, attain human happiness through sound thinking and correct reasoning. It is the duty of the parents to train their children for good conduct by different methods of discipline such as flogging, if necessary, or rebuke if availing or promises of favour or enjoyment which they like or warning of punishment which they fear.[11]

Ibn Miskawaih's on the Education of the child[12]

The child should be trained to give preference to others over himself in food and to be content with what is moderate and frugal in seeking.

He should be taught that the people who wear coloured and embroidered clothes are firstly women who adorn themselves for the sake of men and secondly slaves and servants and that the dress which is not un-becoming of noble and honourable people is white or its like. Thus on being brought up on these teachings and hearing the same from every body around him he should also be prevented from mixing with those who tell him the contrary.

He should be required to learn by heart good traditions and poems which corroborate what he has practised in his education so that by reciting, learning and discussing these ideas become confirmed in him. He would be to put on guard against the study of frivolous poetry and what it contains about love and lovers. For this type of poetry has a strong corrupting influence.

The boy should be praised and honoured for any good trait or any good deed which he may show. If at times he violates what I have described as preferable he should not be reproved for it openly. If he repeats it let him be reproached for it secretly, shown the seriousness of his action and warned against doing that again. For if you accustom him to reproach you will make him impudent.

The training of the child should begin with the formation of good manners in eating. The boy should be made to understand that eating is meant only for health and not for pleasure and that all kinds of food have been created and prepared for use solely to make our bodies healthy and to sustain our life. They should be considered as a medicine with which we remedy hunger and the pain resulting from it.

The boy should have his full meal in the evening for if he takes full meal during the day he will become slow. Furthermore the boy should be forbidden to do anything which he hides or conceals.

He should not be allowed to sleep too long because too much sleep makes him flabby, dulls his mind and deadens his thinking. As for sleep during the day he should never be accustomed to it. Similarly he should not be given a soft bed and any other means of luxury and flabbiness so as to harden his body and to habituate him to rough life.

He should be taught when in company of others not to spit or blow his nose or yawn or cross his legs.

Further he should be trained not to tell lies and never swear whether truthfully or falsely for swearing is disgraceful for men.

He should also be taught to keep silent, to talk sparingly and only to answer question, if he is in the company of older people his duty is to listen to them and to keep silent. He should be forbidden to utter improper speech or talk nonsense.

If the boy is beaten by the teacher he should not cry or ask for intercession of any one for such is the conduct of slaves and those who are weak and feeble.

He should be accustomed not to treat other boys harshly but to show kindness to them and to repay their favour with a bigger one.

He should be made to detest silver and gold and fear them

more than he does lions, snakes, scorpions and serpents for the love of silver and gold is more harmful than poison.

He should be trained to obey parents, teachers and to honour, extol and revere them.

These ideas show that according to Ibn Miskawaih the ethical aspect is very important in the education of the child. The ethics of Ibn Miskawaih as we have already seen was based on the ethics of Plato and Aristotle.

Some of the features of good character as emphasised by Ibn Miskawaih are as follows :

1. The child should be trained to lead a simple life.
2. He should move in the company of good people and should not study frivolous poetry.
3. The training of the child should begin with due attention being paid to good manners of eating.
4. The boy should sleep less and should not be given soft bed and other means of luxury so as to harden his body.
5. The child should be taught that love of gold and silver is detestible.

Besides emphasising good morals and mannners of perennial importance Ibn Miskawaih was rather harsh on young children by denying them luxury and comfort. But we should look at his ideas in the context of the times. The life was very hard for the people and their standard of living was very low. So there was an attempt on the part of the educationists to train the children for the hard life ahead. Similar ideas find an echo in the views of Rousseau on training the children for hard life. However, it is not necessary nowadays that these ideas should be followed very strictly as the conditions of the masses has greatly improved and they can afford better condition of life for their children. The bodies of children can be hardened by participation in sports and games and not by denying them good food and comfort.

Ibn Miskawaih's Theory of Education : His theory of education was based on Aristotelian theory of education which stipulated intellectual, physical and moral education aiming at producing good human beings from the social point of view and achieving eternal happiness and self realisation. Like Plato and Aristotle he believed that education is related to state craft. He, therefore, visualised an education system which could fit the people to perform the duties entrusted to them by the state. Like Aristotle he presented the view that physical education must precede the spiritual and intellectual education. To Ibn Miskawaih the goal of life was to combine the human will with the Divine will. The best preparation for it consisted in making the body an ally rather than an enemy of soul. True education must therefore, minister to the needs of the body no less than the aspirations of the soul. Thus asceticism was entirely unacceptable to him. The need of religious education is, however, apparent because of his professed aim of combining the human will and the Divine Will. The aim of religious education was not only to shield against irreligion but for building the conscience of the child.

The psychological basis of Ibn Miskawaih's theory of education was the view that the child is neither naturally good nor bad. He is simply innocent. His mind is like a clean slate at birth on which we may write whatever we want. Then he points out that there are certain powers which unfold themselves as the child grows. The most important of these powers is the sense of shame which the child displays over his uncommendable acts. The first appearance of this power marks the dawn of reason which makes the child distinguish good from bad, true from false and beautiful from ugly. This power can be used for disciplining the child. It is because of this tendency that there is hope of being improved by education. As soon as he succumbs to impudence he cannot benefit from education. The real cause of impudence is the use of force and punishment. Thus he was against use of force and punishment as a corrective. The other powers which appear very early are desires, self assertion and reason. The child's first desire is for food and dress. He should be taught to be moderate. Because too much food is injurious for health. He should be taught to use as much food as is needed for promoting vigour of the body and relieve him of the pain of hunger. They should be discouraged from fondness for food. Similarly about the dress they should be taught that it is meant for protecting the body from the rigours of climate so they should use only simple dress and should not develop love for gaudy dress. The other important power which appears in the child is self expression. This power finds expression in self display and pride. So adequate opportunities for the expression of this tendency be provided but the unhealthy tendency of taking pride in one's food, clothes and riches must be curbed because it may lead to despising the ill-fed and ill-clothed people. So side by side the display of self assertion they should be taught to obey parents and elders, to be kind, magnanimous, courteous and polite. Lastly there is the reasoning power. It is in fact the educator of desire and self assertion. It's corrective function however depends on the knowledge of the Divine Law. Hence it is necessay that as soon as the child begins to exhibit the power of discrimination oral instruction must begin. He must absorb correct ideas from religious traditions. The final phase on religious education is reached when the child grows up and he is in need of submitting before the will of God. Education at this stage should comprise the study of Holy Law followed by principles of ethics, politics, logic, mathematics and metaphysics. The aim of ethics and metaphysics should be to make the child understand God.

References

1. Ibn Miskawaih : *Tahdhib al-Akhlāq* (English translation entitled *Refinement of Character*) by C.K. Zurayak, Beirut 1968. Preface, pp. xii-xiii.
2. *Ibid.*, pp. 8-15.
3. *Ibid.*, p. 15.
4. *Ibid.*, pp. 17-19.
5. *Ibid.*, pp. 18-19.
6. *Ibid.*, pp. 36-37.
7. *Ibid.*, p. 36.
8. *Ibid,*, p. 30.
9. *Ibid.*, p. 30.
10. *Ibid.*, p. 31.
11. *Ibid.*, p. 32.
12. *Ibid.*, pp. 51-55.

CHAPTER V

EDUCATIONAL PHILOSOPHY OF AL-GHAZZĀLĪ

Background : Al-Ghazzālī (1058-1111 A.D.) was one of the most important thinkers of Islam from our point of view. The period in which al-Ghazzālī lived was marked by ferment in religious thought as well as in political conditions. The great Caliphate was disintegrating and new principalities were coming into existence. The essential unity of Islam was broken because various sects and factions which were always fighting among themselves. They had their origin in politics as well as religion. The rulers of the new principalities were also at logger-heads for achieving supremacy over the other. The Buwehids of Persia overpowered the Abbasid Caliphs and ruled on their behalf. The Buwehids were Shi'ās and in their zeal for spreading their ideology persecuted non-Shi'ās. They patronised the Mu'tazila who preached all sort of heresies. Later on the Seljūqs attacked them and freed the Abbasid Caliphs from the grip of the Buwehids but in turn brought them under their own control. As they professed Sunnī ideology they suppressed heresy and un-Islamic views. In Egypt at that time another sect of Shi'ās, the Fātimids preached Isma'īlī doctrines who according to Sunnīs were heretical and un-Islamic. The Seljūqs curbed their power. Another danger which the world of Islam faced was from the Christians who defeated the Seljūqs and occupied Jerusalem. It was in this background that al-Ghazzālī born and bred in true Islamic environment found himself face to face with great challenges. He made a determined bid to fight the forces of disruption in Islam at the intellectual plane. He adopted teaching as his profession and imparted instruction in Islamic sciences. He wrote a number of books on refutation of the philosophical doctrines as well as on refutation of other heretical doctrines. His most important work was on Islamic science i.e. *Iḥya 'Ulūm al-din* which was written in order to preserve the Islamic sciences from destruction at the hands of the heretics.

Before discussing al-Ghazzāli's views in greater detail it is worthwhile to trace briefly the life history of this great scholar of Islam.

Life Sketch of al-Ghazzali

Abul Ḥāmid Moḥammad surnamed al-Ghazzālī was born in 1058 A.D. at Ṭūs in Khurāsān. His father was dervesh. Naturally the life of his father must have exerted a lot of influence on the mind of al-Ghazzālī. The first teacher to whom his early education was entrusted was a Ṣūfī. Then al-Ghazzālī went to Nayasabūr to study under the well known divine Imām al-Ḥarmain in Niẓamia Academy. He soon became the most distinguished of Imām's pupils. His studies covered an extensive range of subjects particularly Theology, Fiqh, Philosophy, Logic and Mysticism. From Nayasabūr al-Ghazzālī went to the court of Niẓāmul Mulk the Vazier of the Seljūq king Malik Shāh who appointed him the President of the Niẓāmia Academy of Baghdad. Here al-Ghazzāli established his reputation as a teacher of great eminence. After some time Al-Ghazzālī felt spiritually disturbed because of the chaotic multiplicity of creeds, sects and beliefs. He became a skeptic. He therefore made up his mind to explore these beliefs and sects to find the truth. At last he left Baghdād and spent about ten years roaming about in Syria, Ḥijāz and other places in search of peace of mind. It was through transcendental experience that he came to the conclusion that knowledge gained by senses cannot be relied upon. About reason he thought that it is also faulty. He studied theology and philosophy but was not satisfied. Then he was attracted towards Ṣūfism. He got some satisfaction in it as it renounces the material world and preaches devotion to God. At last he came to the conclusion that intuition is the only way for understanding the truth. He then decided to serve Islam and to revive Islamic ideals and fight heresy and skepticism. It was at this time that the king of Nayāsabūr requested him to join the Academy at Nayāsabūr as teacher. He accepted the offer and started teaching at the Academy. After some time he left it, went to Ṭūs where he founded a Madrasa where he taught Fiqh and Taṣawwuf till his death. It was during this period that he wrote the book *Iḥya 'Ulūm al-dīn* (Revivifying of the sciences of faith). Al-Ghazzālī had many other books to his credit e.g. *Maqāsid al-Falasifa* (Aims of Philosophers), *Tahāfut al-Falasifa* (Refutation of Philosophers), *Munqidh min al-Ḍalāl* (Saviour from Darkness), *Mīzān al-'Amal* (on Ethics), etc. We get a glimpse of the educational ideals of al-Ghazzālī from his book *Iḥya 'Ulūm al-dīn.*

Al-Ghazzālī's concept of Knowledge

Al-Ghazzālī believed that man has been endowed by God with all the powers needed for the acquisition of knowledge of Ultimate Reality. This knowledge was derived through the intellect which is the innate rational faculty of man and which distinguishes him from animals. The highest form of knowledge is spiritual knowledge. This knowledge depends on intuition as well as effort. When man acquires this knowledge it is necessary that man should control his lower faculties such as appetites, anger and self-assertion. If man yields before them then he comes down to the level of the brutes. Al-Ghazzālī further says that knowledge has two aspects—the theoretical and the practical. The theoretical knowledge helps in the comprehension of transcendental world *i.e.* knowledge of God and mystries of creation etc. Thus it includes metaphysics and the sciences. The practical knowledge is complementary to theoretical knowledge, it's active function lies in human conduct. The sciences are of two kinds *viz.* the religious Sciences (Shar'īyya) and the intellectual sciences or philosophy ('Aqliyya). The study of religious sciences is obligatory (Farḍ 'Ain) for all Muslims while the study of philosophy and other sciences is obligatory for some people (Farḍ Kifaya). The study of the former is obligatory for all the Muslims because they are the means of purification of soul which is the ultimate end. The study of the latter is not binding on every Muslim if there are sufficient people to study these sciences to satisfy the needs of the community.

Al-Ghazzālī's Concept of Human Nature

Al-Ghazzālī believed like Plato that man possesses appetites, anger and intellect which have their origin in the natural principle such as appetite is derived from the beastly, anger from ferocious and intellect from the divine elements of his nature. Here are the words of al-Ghazzālī : "There are four natures of men : 1. Beastly, 2. Animal, 3. Develish, 4. Angelic. Anger is the sign of beastly nature. Domination of appetites can be attributed to animal nature. The develish nature is exhibited in deceit, fraud, conspiracy etc. The angelic nature is discernible in the desire for service, worship of God and doing good to all. These four natures are centred in soul. If man follows the animal nature he behaves like a pig or dog. If he follows the devil he becomes deceitful and fraudulent. If he controls the above evils he is endowed with divine qualities such as wisdom, knowledge and faith.[2]

Al-Ghazzālī, however, points out that the animal nature of man like appetites and anger are not without any good uses but they should not be allowed to dominate. The appetites, for example, urge the body to obtain what is needed by the body while anger is used for repelling what is harmful to it. Man is distinguished from the animals in possessing the reflecting power of the mind. This power controls and regulates the natural propensities. Thus mind has supremacy over matter. Mind is the source of all human activities. In addition to this man also possesses another quality which enables him to attain perfection. This is the will power which depends on intellect. About the will power al-Ghazzālī says : "When man can understand from his intellect the result of any action and knows what will bring good then grows in his mind the will to obtain that good and to do that act."[3]

Al-Ghazzālī further says that there is a continuous conflict between the intellect and the animal nature. The animal nature revolts against the intellect and try to overcome it. The intellect because of the divine element in it fight these forces and tries to control and divert them to the right path. If the intellect succeeds in making them completely submissive to itself then man achieves the state of abstinence and piety. If on the other hand the intellect is overcome by animal nature he falls prey to wickedness, impudence and hatred etc.[4]

Moral and Ethical Philosophy of al-Ghazzālī

Al-Ghazzālī's ethical philosophy is based on the theory that the fundamental elements of human nature *i.e.* reason, self-assertion and appetition must work together in harmony, observing the golden mean and under the control of reason. In this case virtues are produced. If on the other hand baser elements are not under proper control of reason then vices are produced. Further, he says that virtuous life is characterised by supremacy of the rational self and complete surrender to the will of God. Every act of a virtuous man is motivated by the desire to please God and to be near Him. Al-Ghazzālī divides virtues into two broad categories :[5] 1. Those which are means to higher ends such as repentence, patience, fear of God and piety etc. 2. Those which are means as well as ends such as Absolute reliance on God (*Tawakkul*) and thankfulness to God (*Shukr*). In another classification he divides virtues into five groups :[6] 1. Virtues connected with the world of things *e.g.* repentence, poverty and patience. 2. Virtues related to present state of the working of the heart *e.g.* meditation (*Murāqiba*), mortifying the self (*Mujahāda*) and punishing the self (Mu'aqaba). 3. Virtues connected with singleness of purpose. This means that the heart is completely purified and nothing remains in the heart except the desire for communion with God. 4. Virtues connected with the future relation of man with God such as fear of God and hope from God. 5. Reliance on God (*Tawakkul*) and thankfulness to God (*Shukr*).[7]

Vices :[8] Vices are just the opposite of virtues. They are unethical forms of the natural propensities of man. They are harmful because they engender love of world at the expanse of spiritual development. Love of the world is the root of all vices. Al-Ghazzali classifies vices into various groups : (1) Vices connected with physical organs such as stomach and tongue. The vice of stomach is gluttony and vice of tongue is abuse slandering etc. (2) Vices connected with propensities of anger and self-assertion such as malice, envy, pride etc.

(3) Vices consciously committed to mislead people such as hypocracy. (4) Vices of wilful self-deception such as pride.

Social virtues : Now reverting of the topic of virtue we will take up the social virtues which aim at love of God's noblest creation *i.e.* human beings. Al-Ghazzālī keeps before the example of prophet Mohammad (Peace be on him). He takes into account the laws of Islam in social relations such as dealing with friends, neighbours, servants etc. These relations are based on justice and beneficience.

Religious virtues : Al-Ghazzālī's ethics is built on Islamic ethics which is a complete code of life bearing on every phase of human activity and every aspect of human conduct. All Islamic laws, social, political and others are religious laws. They all aim at the realisation of the ideal of obedience to God and His laws. The observance of various religious duties such as cleaning of body, prayer, fasting, charity (Zakāt) and Ḥajj are some of the religious values which should be aimed at by all Muslims. Offering of prayer is essential because it washes away sins just as water washes away dirt from the body. The prophet said : "Prayer saves man from what is obscene and evil." Prayer gives an opportunity of communion with God and to humble oneself before God and to concentrate on Him. Giving of alms (zakāt) is reckoned as one of the pillars of Islam. It is mentioned in the Qur'ān along with prayer *e.g.* "Pray and pay Zakāt." The recalcitrants have been warned : "But to those who hoard up gold and silver and spend not for the pleasure of God, announce to them tidings of grevious torment." Pilgrimage (Ḥajj) gives an opportunity of complete surrender to the will of God if it is performed in the right spirit. In short it may be said that the performance of religious duties is the basis of virtuous life aiming at the purification of heart and seeking nearness to God and love of God. The criterion of man's love for Him is to prefer Him to the world and what it contains.

Character formation : Al-Ghazzālī holds the view that man has two aspects—the physical and the spiritual. Character is related to the spiritual aspect. Further character formation depends on interest tendencies both voluntary as well involuntary. Another important thing which influences character is that some men are born with mental power which can help them to acquire control over baser elements of their nature such as self-assertion and appetition etc. In others these elements are stronger so they need great effort of the will to achieve perfection of character. Character is also affected by unconscious imitation of those with whom one associates. As pointed out earlier the interaction of reason, self-assertion and appetition produces vices and virtues. These qualities make or mar character. Self-assertion functioning under proper control of reason produces the virtues of generosity, courage and self-respect. If self-assertion is not properly guided by reason it leads to cowardice, lavishness etc. If appetition exists in right relationship with reason it promotes chastity, temperance, modesty and patience. If it is not properly guided by reason it produces vices like gluttony, shamelessness and extravagance.

Al-Ghazzālī on Education of Children

Al-Ghazzālī's views on education and instruction of children which are illustrative of his concept of character training comprising promotion of good manners and ethical and moral qualities under the guidance of teachers and parents are reproduced below :

The education of children is an important duty of the parents. The child is a trust in the hands of the parents. His heart is like a bright jewel and soft like a candle free from any impression. It is soft like clay in which every seed can grow. If he is given good training of character and conduct he will surely follow the truth when grown up and will attain happiness in both the worlds which will be shared by his parents and teachers. Lack of proper education ruins the child. In his sins too the parents as well as teachers will have a share. Parents should train their children in good conduct, keep them away from bad company, luxurious habits, delicious dishes and beautiful clothes.

The care of the child must commence from the very beginning. First of all he must be suckled by a virtuous woman. For the milk becomes a part of child's system, nourishes his body and builds up his mind and influences it for better or for worse.

When the boy reaches the age of discretion still greater care is to be taken. The appearance of the sense of shame marks the beginning of discrimination between good and evil and the dawn of reason.

The child's first desire is for food. He should be taught eating manners. He must begin with the name of Allah, use his right hand, eat what is near him. He should not look greedily at any one who is eating. He should be taught to avoid haste in eating, to chew his food well, not to take it in morsels in quick succession, and not to smear his clothes and hands with the food and that he should not over eat. Some time he should eat course bread in order to get used to it. Those who eat moderately must be praised before him. He should be taught to give away food to others and learn self-sacrifice.

The boy should be taught to prefer plain clothes to coloured or silk dress. Those dressed in silk and in gaudy colours should be despised before him. He should not be allowed to mix with them.

He should be sent to school and taught the Qur'ān and the Ḥadīth and the stories of pious people so that the love of these may take root in his heart. He must not be allowed to read love poetry and to meet persons who consider it a means of cleverness and wit. Such poetry can only sow the seed of evil in him.

Reward the boy if he does something good and praise him before the people for it. He will be pleased and encouraged. Overlook his undesirable acts when they are first committed. Do not let out his secrets. Do not scold him frequently. If he gets accustomed to it he will become insensitive to it, would stick to his fault and acquire evil ways. The father should talk to him considerately and seldom scold him. The mother should also stop him from evil things. She should remind him of father's warning.

He must not be given chance of forming the habit of sleeping in the day time as it causes laziness. He must not be stopped from sleeping at night. He should not sleep on soft bed. Thus the desires for comfort in the matter of bed, dress, and food must not be allowed to develop.

A child must not be allowed to do anything in secret for what one does in secret is that which he considers too bad to be done before the people. If he forms the habit of doing everything openly he will not do anything bad.

He must not boast among his companions of his fathers possessions nor should be proud of what he eats, wears or possesses.

He should not accept things from others. If he is rich he should be advised to spend on others. If he is poor he should be told that to accept things from others is a mark of greed and humiliation. Love and greed for gold and silver must be checked.

He must be taught how to sit properly and speak little. He should show respect to elders and make room for them.

He must be prevented from saying what is nonsense, obscene and indiscreet. He must not be allowed to associate with those who have bad habits for bad habits are easily contracted in bad company. In educating the boys the fundamental thing is to shield them from the society of evil men.

If the teacher beats a boy the boy should not make much fuss over it nor seek anybody's intervention but be patient. He must be told that to bear punishment and pain with patience is an act of bravery. It is the women and the slave who weep and cry.

After returning from school he should be allowed to play. If a boy is not allowed to play his heart is depressed and his intellect becomes dull. His life becomes bitter and he begins to find excuses for not learning. He must be taught to obey his parents, teachers, instructors and every one who is older than himself.

When he reaches the age of discretion he should be taught cleanliness and offering of prayer.

In Ramaḍān he should be induced to fast on certain days. He must be taught religious laws according to need.

His training should create in him abhorrence of theft, misappropriation, lying, obscenity and similar vices.

After educationing the child on above lines he should be initiated, during adolescence, into the significance deeper spirit and the meaning of religion. The futility and transitory nature of the worldly joys should be impressed upon him. The pleasure of God should always regulate his desire and motivate him.

The ideas of al-Ghazzālī on the education of children are more or less on the same lines as formulated by Ibn Miskawaih. Like Ibn Miskawaih he emphasises character training as the main aim of education. Character training included promotion of ethical and moral qualities such as obedience to parents, teachers and elders and abhorrence of theft, lying and obscenity. He was against mixing of young children with people and children of bad character. He was against teaching love poetry to young children. He cautioned the parents against children desiring for comfort in matter of food, dress and bed etc. He also emphasised development of self respect and avoidance of pride and love of riches.

Al-Ghazzālī entrusted the responsibility of the training of the children to parents and teachers and they were held responsible for the shortcomings of the children under their charge. He, however, says that they should not be too harsh on the child and should not scold him too often because frequent scolding and beating makes him indolent. Thus al-Ghazzālī's ideas on discipline are psychologically sound.

Aims of Education according to al-Ghazzālī

In the light of the philosophical and ethical ideas of Ghazzālī the ultimate aim of education was the development of character which besides including the promotion of moral and ethical qualities such as obedience, humility, simplicity and abhorrence of vices like pride, love of wealth and lying meant complete surrender to the will of God, reliance on God and thankfulness to Him.

Education should make the child aware of the laws of Islam through the study of the Qur'ān and the Ḥadith. This will give him theoretical knowledge of Islam but on this is not sufficient. Education should habituate the child to offer prayers regularly and to observe fast and follow other mandatory laws of Islam. Thus education should make the child firm in religious beliefs otherwise he will be led astray.

Content of Education

Al-Ghazzali's views on the courses of studies are discussed in detail on page 16. His emphasis on religious and moral education gives the impression that he was against intellectual sciences like natural sciences and philosophy but this is not the correct assessment. He in fact recommended the study of intellectual subjects like philosophy, logic and other sciences in the Islamic syllabus. He regretted that in his days religious subjects were given greater attention and secular subjects like agriculture and medicine were ignored.

Method of Teaching

Al-Ghazzālī laid great stress on the preparation of the lesson by the teacher. He also emphasised that the teachers should have a thorough knowledge of the subject which they teach. Another point towards which he drew the attention of the teachers was that they should develop the lesson with the cooperation of the pupils as this will facilitate understanding of the lesson by the pupils. He also pointed out that the new knowledge should be related with the knowledge already possessed by the pupils. He also cautioned the teachers against presenting complex and difficult subject matter in the beginning and asked them to proceed from simple to complex because if the complex subject matter is taken up in the beginning then the child will be confused and will loose interest in the subject. Al-Ghazzālī also pointed out that the teacher should have full knowledge of the abilities, capacities and interests of the child and plan his teaching accordingly.

Duties of Students and Teachers : Al-Ghazzālī demanded from the students moral and ethical qualities of the highest order. He expected the student to purify his self from low habits and evil qualities, because knowledge is a prayer of heart and is divine and it enters only pure hearts. He advised them to serve all relations with the world. He should not be proud of his knowledge and should not make a show of his learning before his teacher. He should abide by the precepts of the teacher as a patient follows the instructions of the physician. Al-Ghazzālī decried that some students are too proud to study under an obscure teacher. He advised the students not to care whether the teacher is famous or not. The student should be like a soft rock which taken in all the rain which falls on it.

Regarding teachers he says that they should have love and sympathy for his pupils and should be an embodiment of good manners and morals so that the children may emulate his example and thus indirectly he should mould their character. The teacher should be perfectly honest in his profession and should not discriminate between rich and poor students. The teacher should take into account the intellectual level of the student before teaching and must guard against teaching a matter which is beyond their comprehension. The teacher has to practise what he preaches.

References

1. Al-Ghazzālī : *Ihya 'Ulūm al-dīn* (Egypt 1933) part I, pp. 13-15.
2. *Ibid.*, (English translation by Fazlul Karim, Vol. III, pp. 10-11).
3. *Ibid.*, p. 9.
4. Umaruddin : *Ethical Philosophy of al-Ghazzālī*, p. 138.
5. *Ibid.*, p. 175.
6. *Ibid.*, p. 175; see also al-Ghazzālī : *Ihya 'Ulūm al-dīn*, English translation by Fazlul Karim, Vol. IV, Chapter II.
7. Umaruddin : *op. cit.*, p. 159.
8. Al-Ghazzālī : *Ihya Ulūm al-dīn* English translation by Fazlul Karim Vol. II, Chapter II, pp. 145-17.
9. Umaruddin : *op. cit.*, p. 139.
10. Al-Ghazzālī : *Iḥya 'Ulūm al-dīn* Cairo, Vol. III, pp. 62-63.

Chapter VI

EDUCATIONAL PHILOSOPHY OF IBN KHALDŪN

Ibn Khaldūn was a great scholar of Islamic sciences as well as many other sciences such as history, geography, politics and education. He was the founder of the philosophy of history and a precursor of sociology. Here we are concerned with his views on education. Ibn Khaldūn discussed the educational process in the perspective of the development of society. He expounded his theory of education in the framework of Islamic society and focussed his attention on education from a religious and ethical point of view but at the same time he highlighted the sociological point of view also.

Life sketch : Abdur Raḥman Ibn Khaldūn was born in Tunis on 27th May 1332. He was a descendant of the Banū Khaldūns of Spain who later migrated to Tunis. Ibn Khaldūn began his education with learning the Qur'ān by heart. He was fortunate in having his early education conducted by an eminent teacher of Tunis. He took keen interest in law, tradition, language, grammar and poetry. Later he studied logic, philosophy, theology and other Islamic sciences. After attaining the age of 21 he joined the service of the king of Tunis but soon left it. In 1354 he was invited to Fez for secretaryship of Abu Enan but after a few years he left this job also. In 1362 he went to the court of Sultan of Granada and lived there for two years and then returned to Africa. This time too he held high positions and then went to Qalat b. Salama and resided there till 1378. It was here that Ibn Khaldūn started writing his world famous history entitled *Kitāb al-'Ibar wa dīwān al-Mubtadā wa'l Khabar.* In 1382 he set out for Mecca but stopped at Cairo to deliver lectures at

Al-Azhar University. At Cairo he was appointed Qaḍī in 1384. He held this post till his death in 1406. Ibn Khaldūn's fame rests on the *Muqaddima* (*Prolegomena*) which was written as an introduction to the above named book. The *Muqaddima* contains a systematic treatment of the philosophy of history. Besides this it contains his views on all aspects of state and society which included a detailed account of education as well.

Ibn Khaldūn's Concept of Thinking Process

Ibn Khaldūn says that the ability to think is man's special natural gift which God created exactly as He created other creatures. It is the action and motive in the soul. At times thinking means the beginning of orderly and well arranged human activity, at other times it means the beginning of knowledge of something that has not been available. This ability is directed toward some objective whose two extremes he has pursued and to affirm or deny it. In almost no time he recognises the middle term which combines the two extremes. The faculty of reflective thinking is the source of knowledge. It is this faculty which distinguishes man from animals. It is this faculty which makes him work for livlihood and directs his attention to God. This faculty is of three types: (i) Discerning intelligence which gives man an understanding of the order of things as he finds them in human society. (ii) Experimental intelligence which enables man to be receptive to opinions and teaches him rules of conduct. (iii) Speculative intelligence which gives insight about the general idea of things existing according to species, classes and their primary and secondary causes. This type of intelligence is found in dwellers of cities. It is the result of certain social functions and manifestations peculiar to city life such as leisure for contemplation.

Ibn Khaldūn's Concept of Hierarchy of Knowledge

The classification of knowledge according to Ibn Khaldūn has been given elsewhere. But it may be pointed out here that he laid great stress on Ulum Naqliyya *i.e.* the Qur'ān, interpretation of the Qur'ān, Tradition, Jurisprudence and speculative theology which are wanted *per se.*[2] Then there were Ulum Aqliyya such as philosophy and the physical sciences. Lastly there was another group of sciences which are auxiliary to the above mentioned sciences such as philology is auxiliary to religious sciences, logic is auxiliary to philosophy, speculative theology and jurisprudence. Ibn Khaldūn warns the scholar that they should study the sciences that are wanted *per se* in greater detail. It will clarify their ideas but the auxiliary sciences should not be in greater detail as it will lead away from their main purpose of understanding the sciences they want to study.[3] Hence the sciences that are wanted *per se* suffer. He, however, says those who have a mind to go more deeply into them may choose such a course for themselves.

Aims of Education : Ibn Khaldūn believed that the attainment of knowledge was the natural urge of human beings because they possess the power of thinking and reasoning. Further, he believed that reality should be known by revelation and not by intellectual effort as believed by the philosophers. Thus for the Muslims the first condition for knowing the reality was the Qur'ān and the prophet Moḥammad (Peace be on him). This was the crux of Ibn Khaldūn's philosophy of education. He gave it a sociological dimension by relating education with the Islamic society.

The aim of education according to Ibn Khaldūn is to make Muslims firm believers in God through the study of the Qur'ān and the religious sciences. Knowledge of God and faith in Islamic laws will make Muslims know the reality which in turn will lead to good action and possession of good character. Thus the knowledge of Islamic sciences and leading his life according to the tenets of Islam will help him to be a good Muslim and a good member of society.

Content of Education : *Elementary level* : Ibn Khaldūn discusses in detail the different approaches to the course content at the elementary level prevalent in his days in the Islamic countries.[4]

The Maghribī Method is to restrict the education of the children to instruction of the Qur'ān and to practise during the course of instruction, orthography and its problems. They do not teach any other subject such as tradition, Jurisprudence, poetry or Arabic philology until the pupil is skilled in the Qur'ān. The result of this is that Maghribis know the orthography of the Qur'ān better than any other.

In Spain they pay attention to reading and writing but they do not restrict their instruction exclusively to the Qur'ān. They bring other subjects mainly poetry and composition. They give an expert knowledge of Arabic. They do not stress the teaching of the Qur'ān more than any other subject. Abu Bakr al-'Arabī who was an exponent of Spanish system of education emphasises instruction in Arabic poetry because it excells all other branches cultivated by Arabs. So poetry and philology should be taught first. After this the students should be introduced Arithmetic till they master it and at this stage Qur'ān should be introduced. At this stage they will be able to understand Qur'ān, traditions and other religious sciences. But Ibn Khaldūn does not agree with this approach because, he says that if the teaching of the Qur'ān is delayed it is just possible that they may not get an opportunity of learning the Qur'ān because of other preoccupations or may go astray after coming of age. So it is better to start them teaching the Qur'ān at the earliest age so that they may not miss the blessings and reward in the other world resulting from the knowledge of the Qur'ān.

The people of Ifriquia (Tunis) combine instruction of Qur'ān with the teaching of Tradition. They also teach basic scientific norms and certain scientific problems. However, the stress is on imparting knowledge of Qur'ān, acquaintance with various recensions and reading more than anything else. Next they stress hand-writing.

The people of eastern countries have a mixed curriculum. They are concerned with teaching the Qur'ān and other religious books. They do not combine instruction in Qur'ān with instruction in handwriting.

Content of Education

Higher level : Ibn Khaldūn points out the defect of the syllabi of higher education in these words :

The student has to learn a great number of minor treatises and commentaries and super commentaries which were extremely abbreviated. In addition to this he has to study different schools of the subject. Thus the student is lost in superfluities and has to waste a lot of time before he reaches the subject itself. Even after he has read a number of commentaries and super-commentaries he did not learn more than what he would have learnt from a well written book.[5] He cites an example of Maliki Canon Law on which there were many commentaries. Besides reading these commentaries the student has to learn the methods followed at Qairawan, Cordova, Baghdad and Cairo. Another example of overburdening the student is of Arabic philology. The main manual of study was the book of Sibawaih on which there were many commenataries and the methods were of Basra, Kufa, Baghdad and Spain. Rarely did the student grasp all the intricacies involved in this complicated process. And the pity is that all this labour is wasted on an instumental science which is only a tool for the study of other subjects.[6]

On language teaching Ibn Khaldūn says that language is the expression of the intention of the speaker. Expression through language is an act of the tongue originating in the desire to convey the meaning of speech. It is in the tongue that the language must become an established habit. Thus language is nothing but a habit of the tongue which can be firmly established by constant practice. All languages are habits akin to crafts and just as several craft serve different human purposes the language serves the purpose of expressing ideas. A good linguistic habit means that there is no impediment between ideas and understanding. Linguistic habit includes the skills to combine words into sentences so as to express the ideas one wants to express and also the ability to observe the form of composition suitable to the requirement of the situation. So in order to develop eloquence in speech one must have firstly a perfect linguistic habit, secondly, the ability to form sentences and thirdly an ability to suit the composition to the occasion.

On teaching of two or more languages[8] Ibn Khaldūn was of the view that learning of the language is like learning a craft and just as a person who has obtained proficiency in a craft finds it difficult to master another. Similarly if in a person a certain language habit is firmly established he would find it difficult to cultivate and master another. So the second language can be learnt and mastered only if the first and the second languages are spoken and learnt simultaneously. Full mastery of the second language is not possessed by those students who learn it after having formed a habit of the first language.

Method of Teaching: Ibn Khaldūn pointed out that the teacher should first of all know and understand the nature of his pupils and should bear in mind their innate capacities. He should begin the education of the child with simple things and later on should introduce more difficult and complex things. Effective teaching according to him should proceed step by step. The teaching should be done in three stages.[9] In the first stage the fundamental and the principal problems of the subject should be introduced, while doing this the teacher should observe the intellectual potential and his preparedness for understanding the subject. In the second stage difficult and intricate problems should be clarified. At the third stage the teacher should again revise the whole thing so as to leave nothing obscure and vague. He should lay bare all the secrets of the discipline to him. If the student is taught in this way he will attain complete mastery over the subject.

Ibn Khaldūn cautions against confronting the student with obscure details in the beginning. Nothing is more erroneous than this. Here are his words :[10] "We have observed that many teachers are ignorant of this effective method of teaching. They begin their instruction by confronting the student with obscure scientific problems and require him to concentrate on solving them. They think that it is the correct teaching method. In fact they confuse him and he looses all interest in the subject. Thus lack of interest in some subjects is due to faulty teaching and nothing else. They ignore the fundamental principle that receptivity to scientific knowledge and understanding grow gradually."

Another point which is emphasised by Ibn Khaldūn is that the teacher should not introduce problems from other disciplines before the student understands one discipline thoroughly and become fully conversant with it. Further he points out that the student should not be exposed to two disciplines at the same time, since he has to divide his attention from the other subject and is not able to attend to either of them, so he thinks both the subjects difficult and obscure.[11] But if the student is free to study the subject of his choice he can pay undivided attention to it and can master it. Ibn Khaldūn further adds that teaching in one discipline should not be prolonged by teaching it at intervals. This causes the student to forget the things learnt. Thus the interruption disrupts scholarly pursuits which requires continuous and repeated activity.

Organisation : *Discipline* : Ibn Khaldūn was against maintaining discipline by force which was in vogue in those days.[13] He says that severity whether of parents or the teacher injured the moral and intellectual dignity of the student. Severity makes him hate his teachers, his parents, his studies and he resorts to falsehood and deception to escape punishment. These vices in course of time get engrained in him and he looses all his human qualities. He looses his sense of shame and his will to defend himself. Severity produces ignorant, narrow minded and low souled people. He further adds that the students and slaves who are brought up with injustice and tyranny loose their energy. It makes them lazy and induces them to tell lies and to be insincere. Thus they learn trickery and deceipt and this become part of their character and their soul becomes too indolent to acquire virtue and good life. This is true of even a whole race which is denied justice and is persistently persecuted, it is demoralised and falls from the pedestal of humanity. Therefore it behoves the parents and teachers not to be unduly severe with children and students in the matter of education.

Students and Politics.[14] Ibn Khaldūn cautions the students against participation in politics. Because of all the people the students are the least familiar with the ways of politics. They are more concerned with searching the ideas and universals which can be of use in interpretation of general studies but in practical matters they may commit mistakes. Similarly very intelligent persons who are well versed in academic pursuits are not for politics. In politics people of average intelligence who have capacity for practical aspects of things fare much better than are intellectuals because they are not troubled by anology and generalisation. They can be successful as politician.

References

1. Ibn Khaldūn : *Prolegomena* (English translation of *Muqaddima* by Rosenthal, Vol. III, pp. 295-96).
2. *Ibid.*, pp. 298-299.
3. *Ibid.*, pp. 299-300.
4. *Ibid.*, pp. 300-305.
5. *Ibid.*, p. 288.
6. *Ibid.*, p. 289.
7. *Ibid.*, p. 342.
8. *Ibid.*
9. *Ibid.*, p. 292.
10. *Ibid.*
11. *Ibid.*, p. 295.
12. *Ibid.*, p. 294.
13. *Ibid.*, pp. 305-306.
14. *Ibid.*, p. 304.

CHAPTER VII

EDUCATIONAL IDEAS OF SOME MUSLIM PHILOSOPHERS AND EDUCATIONAL THINKERS

In addition to the educational thinkers discussed in detail in the proceeding chapters there were others who held important views on education such as al-Fārābī, Ibn Sīna, Ikhwān al-Ṣafa etc. who merit our attention. There were still others who wrote tractates on education particularly at the elementary level such as Ibn-Suhnūn and al-Zarnujī who will also find a place in this chapter.

Educational ideas of al-Jāḥiẓ (IXth Century)

Al-Jaḥiẓ in his *al-Bayān* writes about teachers which is one of the earliest view on the subject.[1] He classified teachers into three classes *viz.* those who teach children of poor people, those who teach children of higher classes and finally those who teach the princes. He himself was the teacher of the sons of al-Mutawakkil.

Al-Jāḥiẓ gives some important suggestions on teaching method and the subjects to be taught. He says that the children should not be over burdened with rules of grammar. They should be taught in such a way that they may avoid the blunders and pitfalls committed by ordinary people while reading or speaking. Anything more than this essential knowledge is mere superfluity and the time spent on it could be more profitably utilised in learning things of greater importance such as proverbs, pithy sayings and good expression. Al-Jaḥiẓ further says that the young pupil should be taught arithmetic without bothering about geometry or surveying, the young learner should learn good composition in familiar words and phrases and should study the works of accomplished writers in order to grasp the sense rather the mere meaning.[2]

Educational ideas of Ibn-Suhnūn

Ibn-Suhnūn (IXth Century) lived at Qairawān and taught in the mosque of Ugaba and also in his house. His short treatise *Adab al-Mu'allimīn* was perhaps the earliest book devoted to elementary education.[2] The book opens with a brief reference to apostelic traditions on learning and teaching of the Qur'ān. Ibn-Suhnūn recommended the learning and teaching of the Qur'ān at an early age for it would be mixed with the blood and flesh of the scholar conforming to the famous maxim that learning in tender age is as effective as inscribing on stone. About the courses of studies he says that the teachers are expected to teach reading, writing and grammatical analysis of the Qur'ān, philosophy, poetry, history of the Arabs, oratory, arithmetic, morals, ablution and prayers. Of this list only the Qur'ān and the rituals are obligatory while the rest are either voluntary or subject to conditions. In teaching the Qur'ān, he says that the pupils should not start with a given *Ṣura* before mastering the one before it. The children should be able to write it, parse it and memorise it. Pupils may dictate to each other but the teacher must check the dictation.

On remuneration to teachers Ibn Suhnūn says that in his days there was the general practice of giving remuneration to teachers teaching the Qur'ān or secular subjects. But the teachers who received pay were strictly forbidden to accept or solicit gifts from children or to employ them for running errands for them. The teachers were expected to give all their time to teaching while the people were in attendance. The teachers were liable to be punished or stopped from teaching if found deficient or negligent.[3]

On Corporal punishment Ibn Suhnūn says that the teacher who inflicted corporal punishment was condemned. The teacher was, however, allowed to give corporal punishment to the child for misconduct or failure to learn the Qur'ān, if permitted by the father of the child. The punishment was restricted to a maximum of three strokes of cane but not on face or head. In no case was the punishment delegated to a pupil or a prefect. Further, on no account the punishment was to take the form of preventing the child from taking his food or drink.[4]

Educational Ideas of al-Fārābī[5]

About the need of the teaching and the teacher al-Fārābī says that man has been created to attain the highest happiness (his idea of happiness is derived from Aristotle). Man should, therefore, know what happiness is and should make the attainment of happiness as the aim of life. But since human individuals differ in nature and every individual cannot know the secret of happiness, he needs a teacher and a guide. Some people require less guidance and teaching and some need more. Then he goes to define teaching and says : Teaching means creating speculative excellence in nations and cities while upbringing (*Tā'dib*) is the method of creating and developing moral virtues and scientific arts. The purpose of teaching is to make nations and citizens habituated to scientific habit. He points out that speculative sciences are learnt either by kings or leaders (*Imāms*). The speculative sciences should be taught by convincing method *i.e.* the logical method.

The teacher should know what should be imparted to a particular nation and how to make it common to all nations or all people of every city. He should also know what should be taught to the entire nation or city and what to a particular group in a city.

Al-Fārābī speaks of two methods of teaching. First, to engender virtues and practical arts in such a convincing way that the pupil regard them as their own and practise them spontaneously. Second, the teacher should use the method of force which is employed for the disobedient citizen and those who do not move to righteousness on their own. Thus the teachers may be divided into two groups in respect to the above two methods. One group teaching and training those who are obedient and the other group teaching the disobedient.

Al-Fārābī says that the king is the teacher of the nation and the master of the house and the teacher of the people of the house. Then he proceeds to describe the qualities of the king or the Imam which are strikingly the same as we expect from a teacher today. The qualities are as under :[6]

1. Sound health and perfect organs performing their functions with ease and facility in harmony with all faculties.

2. Intelligence and sagacity so as to be able to grasp the intention of the speaker in his particular situation and circumstances.

3. Good memory, so as to retain in his mind all that he understands, sees, hears or perceives.

4. Prudence and talent to understand a problem from the perspective in which it has been presented to him.

5. Eloquence, so that his tongue may assist him in expressing in a perfect manner all that he has in his mind.

6. Devotion to education and learning, submission to receive knowledge with ease and without any annoyance.

7. Avoidance of drink and sex, avoidance of play and dislike for pleasure caused by these.

8. Friendliness towards truthful persons and contempt for falsehood.

9. Bigness of heart, loving nobility and natural magnanimity without any trace of meanness.

10. Indifference to dirham and dinars and other form of wealth.

11. Devotion to justice and just people, abhorrence of injustice and oppression.

12. Strong resolution, courage and promptness without any sign of fear or weakness.

Educational Ideas of Ibn Sīnā[7]

Ibn Sina discussed the problems relating to education in his books namely *Tadbīrul Manzil*, the *Qānūn* and *al-Shifa*. These books contain his views on upbringing of the child, children's welfare and to various types of education respectively.

Ibn Sina's views on up-bringing and training of the child are as follows :

The father should have a good name for the child. Then he must find out for him a nurse physically and morally sound. As soon as the child is weaned the father should take interest in building up child's character and in guarding him against undesirable habits and bad companions. Moderation should be observed upto sixth year. The child should not be deprived of those things which he likes and should not be compelled to accept those things which he dislikes so that his mental and moral faculties may attain perfection and at the same time his physical energies develop freely. The child otherwise will become irritable, melancholy or coward and will consequently fell sick or become dull and will have no zest in his work because body and mind influence each other.

When the child attains the age of six the parents should send him to school and keep him engaged in acquiring knowledge till he attains the age of fourteen.

The teacher should be religious minded, pious, intelligent, bold, clean and respectable man. He should know how to live in society and be familier with the methods of teaching and training the child and moulding his character.

The teacher should guard the child against bad habits and evil acts and should get him mixed with good class mates. Secondly while bringing up the child he should sometime excite his interest and sometime take him to task. If the latter docs not produce result he should take recourse to corporal punishment. While dealing with the student the teacher should follow the middle course. He should not behave in such a manner that the students do not have the courage to ask questions or to get things explained nor should he display so much leniency that the children become impertinent and pay no attention to the lectures and lessons.

The teacher should also study the child carefully, examine his nature and temperament, test his intelligence that he may be in a position to choose for him the profession and occupation which may suit his talent or intelligence.

The child should not read all alone for he will feel depressed and unhappy. He should be kept along with the children belonging to respectable families.

The school syllabus for the period of eight years should include reading of Qur'ān, religious instruction, study of language and study of verses which contain good morals and decent manners, physical exercises as well as technical training *i.e.* arts and crafts.

The child should not be occupied wholly with reading, he should spare some time for physical exercises.

The child should be equipped in arts and crafts in which he has received training to enable him to cultivate the habit of earning his living.

The educational ideas of Ibn Sīnā may be summarised as under :

1. The children should be guarded against evil persons having bad character. They should be kept away from all that is obscene and undesirable and should live in the company of virtuous people. This shows that the moral aim was very important according to Ibn Sīnā. With this end in view he emphasised the teaching of Qur'ān, Ḥadīth and Fiqh. In addition to this the whole curriculum was geared to the moral end for example only those stories were to be taught to the children which speak of decent manners and good morals. He should not be taught those stories and fragments of poetry which go against religion and are sources of disorder and corruption.

2. The education of the child should be according to his ability and intelligence. For this purpose it was incumbent upon the teacher to know the nature of the child, his likes and dislikes and his aptitude.

3. Learning of arts and crafts was essential for every student so that they may earn their living by practising a craft in which they had got the training.

Ibn Sīnā's ideas on ethical role of education were quite similar to those of his contemporary Ibn Miskawaih. Ibn Miskawaih was, however, against the teaching of craft because he was under the influence of Plato and Aristotle who thought that work by hand is meant for slaves and not for the elite.

Educational ideas of Ikhwān al-Ṣafā[8]

The Ikhwān say that as soon as the child is born he comes under the influence of the social factor for four complete years during which he reaches a certain stage of intelligence and comprehension. After the fourth year the child begins to acquire habits, knowledge, doctrines, crafts and hobbies by imitation.

The children are apt to use an anology characteristic of them. They believe that their parents are perfect, the conditions prevailing in their house are models for all the conditions elsewhere. In practical skill the children are more apt to master the art, science and craft of their parents.

As regards knowledge the I<u>kh</u>wān say that the knowledge of the knower is the abstract knowledge which lies hidden in his soul which comes out with the help of the teacher. The aptitude to learn belongs to the soul alone. The end of teaching is to purify the souls of the taught and to give them correct behaviour in order to prepare them for immortality and happiness in the hereafter. A science that does not lead to happiness in the hereafter is useless.

Every soul is potentially learned and the parents and the teachers polish its aptitude and help it to become learned in action. A teacher is absolutely necessary especially to common people.

The brain is able to store simultaneously all kinds of information, however diverse and contradictory they may be since it stores their abstractions only.

Essentially knowledge is never spontaneous, it must be taught and learnt. Knowledge is handed down traditionally through religious leaders—the *Imāms* whose ultimate source of knowledge is the prophet who acquires his knowledge from God by inspiration.

Educational Ideas of Ibn al-Ḥajj[9] (1336 A.D.)

Ibn al-Ḥajj's ideas are more or less borrowed from al-<u>Gh</u>azzālī and Ibn Miskawaih. He emphasises good manners and morals like them. Ibn al-Ḥajj says : The mind of the boy is *tabula rasa* receptive of any impression. If he grows up accustomed to do what is right he will be fortunate in this world and the next while his parents and the teachers will share the reward.

The father has the duty of training his child in upright ways and saving him from bad companions. He must not let him grow fond of show and luxury lest he waste his life in seeking them. As soon as the child begins to observe greater watchfulness is needed. This is the time of the beginning of modesty and a sense of shame as the child sees that some acts are proper and others improper. This is a sign of purity of mind.

At first the child is greedy and has to be taught when to eat, to eat slowly and to masticate well, not to dirty his hands and clothes and at times to be content with bread alone. He must learnt to prefer white clothes to silk or coloured garments for these are only for women.

The child should be sent to school when he is seven. There he will learn the Qur'ān, traditions, lives of saints but not poetry about love. He must not meet those who think love poetry elegant and refined.

There should be no sleeping in the day time for this makes the child lazy. The boy must sleep at night but on hard bed. He must be accustomed to walking exercise but he must not walk very fast. He should not boast about his father's wealth, be polite and attentive to all and should not accept presents from other boys. Poor boys should learn that it is disgrace to accept gifts. He should be tanght not to love money for love of money is deadly poison.

Ibn al-Ḥajj's views on the duties and responsibilities of teachers are as follows : The teacher should do all the teaching himself, if necessary he might have an assistant, paid or unpaid or he might employ an older boy to teach the young boys. The teacher must attend to his work and not gossip with passers-by nor leave the school to follow a funeral, for attendance at funeral is no more than commendable whereas teaching is a fundamental duty. The teacher should not use boys as servants. He must not laugh with them nor be too familiar with them. He must be impartial, paying no more attention to the children of the rich than those of the poor. He must not loose his temper nor punish in anger.

Regarding the duties of the parents Ibn al-Ḥajj says : Parents have also their duties. They should not send their children to Christian schools to learn Arithmetic and Geometry since this would be an insult to Islam and encouragement to Christians.

As regards reward and punishment Ibn al-Ḥajj says that the child should be rewarded publicly for what he has done well and his naughtiness should be overlooked and he should not be put to shame. If he repeats the offence he should be punished in private but without nagging for familiarity with reproof breeds contempt. If whipping is necessary it should be proportionate to the tender age and it should not be so severe that the child despises chastisement.

Educational ideas of al-Zarnuji (Burhanuddin) 12th-13th century A.D.

Al-Zarnuji's ideas on education of children are to be found in his book "*Ta'līm al-Muta'lim Tarīq al-Ta'lum*" (Teaching the student how to Study). In this book al-Zarnuji analyses briefly the meaning and scope of education followed by discussion on the nature of knowledge, selection of knowledge, time for attaining knowledge, guidelines for teaching to the beginners, reliance on God and importance of good behaviour etc. The details are given below :

The need for writing the book :—About the need of writing the book al-Zarnuji says : "I have seen that many students fail to achieve knowledge despite effort. The reason for this is that they are not familiar with the principles of learning. This situation has created in me the desire to write down the principles and methods of learning which I have mayself read or heard from my teachers".[11]

Meaning of Knowledge ('Ilm) and its importance

Knowledge is the name of that quality through which the knowable things are known. Many of the qualities of human beings are found in animals also but learning is associated with man only. So it is necessary for man to think about himself and about his environment and try to learn those things which are useful for him and to avoid those things which are harmful. This is called Taqwa (piety), on which depends the glory of the world and the hereafter. As knowledge is noblest desire of a Muslim (man and woman) therefore Islam had made search for knowledge obligatory. The prophet Mohammad (Peace be on him) has said "Search for knowledge is obligatory for men and women both". Al-Zarnuji has divided knowledge into three kinds :

1. That knowledge which is needed for every Muslim.
2. That knowledge which is needed for some people.
3. That knowledge which is never needed by the people and is harmful to them.

The first kind of knowledge is essential for every Muslim. The second kind is essential for those who are suited for attaining that knowledge. If some people devote themselves for the attainment of this knowledge others are exempted from it. The third type of knowledge is prohibited (*i.e.* magic and sorcery).

It is the duty of the state to impart the first kind of knowledge compulsorily. For the sencond only those people should be compelled to study who are most suitable for it and to ban the third type.

The purely religious subjects are Qur'ān, Ḥadi<u>th</u>, Fiqh, Kalām and ethics etc. and the secular subjects are commerce and trade, agriculture, arts and crafts, philosophy, logic, astronomy, mathematics, medicine etc. Out of this list the Qur'ān and Ḥadi<u>th</u> are to be learnt compulsorily while the rest should be optional.[12]

Aim of Education

The aim of education should be to seek the pleasure of God, to remove ignorance from oneself and from other illeterate persons and to work for religion (din). The acquisition of knowledge for status, fame and greatness etc. is undersirable. In other words the aim of education should be purely spiritual and should not be material as it will limit the benefits of learning and will stand in the way of acquisition of knowledge. For the achievement of this noble end it is necessary that the student should abstain from greed and pride and adopt courtesy and chastity otherwise it may lead to humiliation for himself as well as for the whole community of the learned.[13]

Selection of subjects, teachers and fellow students

The study of religion should be given the first place and the unity of God be given priority in it. After this other subjects should be learnt as the need arises. In the selection of books care should be taken that first easier and brief books are studied and after that detailed books. Whichever book is taken it should not be left without finishing it. The same procedure should be followed in other subject. On the selection of teacher the prime consideration should be his erudition and learning, nobility of character and age. In the selection of the class mates, the guiding principle should be their diligence, nobility and intelligence. The company of lazy and talkative students should be avoided.

Respect of knowledge and the teachers :—The respect for knowledge as well as the teacher is essential for the student. The student who has no respect for learning or the learned will either remain ignorant all his life or will not benefit from the blessings of learning. Respect for the teacher is in fact respect for knowledge.

The students should pay attaintion to the following :

1. He should not walk ahead of the teacher.

2. He should not sit where the teacher sits.

3. He should not talk to the teacher without taking permission from him.

4. He should not talk too much.

5. He should not knock at the door of the teacher but should wait for him to come out.

6. He should avoid teacher's displeasure and should desire for his pleasure.

7. He should obey the orders of the teacher excepting those which are against the mandate of God.

8. He should hear teacher's lecture with rapt attention even if he has heard it before. The student who is careless in this respect is not fit for learning.

9. It is necessary for the student to consult the teacher in the selection of the subject, he should not make the decision himself because the teacher has a lot of experience and he knows which subject is suitable for whom.

10. The student should avoid bad manners because knowledge is light which is the quality of God, so bad manners and knowledge cannot be combined.[14]

Consistency is essential for the student. One cannot attain knowledge without constant effort. One should avoid laziness as it is a great calamity. The lazy man is always sorry. The student who is not alert in search of knowledge is in fact ignorant of the blessings of knowledge. The ignorant is dead even if alive and the learned is alive even after death. Too much eating is sometimes the cause of laziness. The student should eat less.

The lesson :—The lesson for the beginner should be such as it may be learnt by repeating twice. The increase should be gradual. Repetition of the lesson is essential. The lesson should be taught orally. Then the student should write down the lesson himself after he has understood it well whether with the help of the teacher or by reading it repeatedly or by thinking over it again and again.

The discussion method :—The students should discuss important problems among themselves but they should take care that they observe norms of justice and possess self control and avoid shouting at each other because it may lead to losing sight of the real purpose of discussion. So discussion with the express objective of defeating the adversary is prohibited. A discussion should be entered into in the spirit of learning something new.

It is necessary for the student to be ready to learn from every one. Once some one asked Abu Yusuf about the secret of his achieving the great status in learning. He replied I never hesitated to learn from anyone and was never miserly in giving the benefit of learning to others.

Earning a living :—There is no enmity between earning a living and learning. If needed the student should earn his living while studying. Poverty should not be an excuse for not learning. In old days education comprised firstly of arts and craft which was followed by theoretical knowledge. The student should place complete reliance on God during student life and should not bother for earning a living. The person who is absorbed in provision of good food and dress can never get the time for studies. He should curtail worldly desires. One of the method for achieving this end is to undertake educational travel and should be ready to bear all the trouble and inconveniences with fortitude.

Qualities of teachers :—The teacher should be an adviser to the student and should not be envious. He should possess the quality of forbearance and patience because the opposite of these qualities are the root cause of enmity. The teacher should always be ready to help the student.

Desirable qualities of students :—The student should be diligent, perseverent and ambitious. In the pursuit of knowledge he should enlist the cooperation of his teacher and fellow students and patrons. The student should not waste time. The best period for the pursuit of knowledge is adolescence and youth. As this period is transitory it is necessary to utilise it to the maximum and not to waste it. Federation should be observed in the pursuit of knowledge and in no case it should be imposed on the will with ruthlessness, because this may lead to weakening of the desire for learning and hatred for learning.

The student should be ambitious. The aims of the ambitious are very high while those of the defeatists are low. Ambition combined with action leads to perfection of knowledge. The student should abstain from impiety because attainment of knowledge is easier for the pious and also more beneficial. Under piety is included eating less, talking less, sleeping less and under impiety comes taking food in the market, back-biting, sitting in the company of talkative people, bad characters and worthless people.

Improvement of memory :—Memory is improved by constant effort for any good cause, paltry fare, prayer and reading of the Qur'ān. Forgetfulness increases with sin, worldly desires, sorrow, and too much work.

Causes which lead to poverty and opulence :—Doing sinful acts, telling lies, sleeping more, disrespect shown to food and elders, laziness in prayers, roaming about in the market place, carelessness about books, miserliness and extravagance lead to poverty. Helping the poor, politeness in speech, cleanliness, offering of prayer with sincerity, respect to elders, helping the poor relatives etc. leads to opulence, so also these qualities lead to longevity.[15]

This study clearly shows that al-Zarnuji emphasised the religious aspect of education. He also emphasised good manners and morals. He says that knowledge is a quality which illumines and provides insight into the secrets of learning. The object of education according to him is to attain the pleasure of God Almightly and the attainment of eternal bliss. For al-Zarnuji education was an aid to 'Taqwa' (piety). conducing to everlasting bliss. He deplores the attitude of 'here and now' and glorified the life to come. "Education" he says, "is bought at a great price and it is pity to waste it on the lowly and perishable world."[16]

References

1. Tibawi : Muslim Education in the Golden Age of Caliphate, Art in *Islamic Culture*, 28 (1954), p. 430.
2. *Ibid.*, p. 431.
3. *Ibid.*, p. 432.
4. *Ibid.*
5. Sarton, *Introduction to the History of Science*, Vol. III, Part II, p. 1767.
6. Sharif, M.M., *History of Muslim Philosophy*, Vol. I, pp. 709-10.
7. Sadiq, I, Avicenna on Education, Art. in *Indo-Iranica*, 1956, 9(4), pp. 71-75.
8. Sharif, M.M., *op. cit.*, Vol. I, p. 712.
9. Tritton : Muslim Education in Middle Ages, Art. in *Muslim World*, 1953 (43), pp. 83-85.
10. Haji Khalifa, *Kashf-ud-Zunūn*, Vol. I, p. 425. See under Talim al-Muta'llim. Sarton, *op. cit.*, Vol. XIII, Part II, pp. 598, 900, 998.
11. Al-Zarnujī, *Talim al-Muta'llim Tarīq al-Ta'lum*, MS. Raza Library, Rampur. Urdu translation by Imtiaz Ali Arshi. Published in *Maqalat-i-Arshi*, Lahore 1970, p. 369.
12. *Ibid.*, pp. 370-71.
13. *Ibid.*, p. 371.
14. *Ibid.*, p. 373.
15. *Ibid.*, p. 375-80.
16. Grunebaum, English Translation of *Ta'lim al-Muta'llim*, New York, 1956, p. 95.

CHAPTER VIII

A SYNOPTIC VIEW OF MUSLIM EDUCATION—AIMS, CONTENT, METHODOLOGY AND ORGANISATION

Aim of Education

The Islamic system of education was based on its value system the basic features of which were embodied in the Qur'ān and the Ḥadīth *e.g.* belief in God, devotion to God, obedience to the commandments of God, as enjoined by the prophet Muḥammad (Peace be on him). The Islamic education system also aimed at stimulating the moral consciousness of the pupils by bringing about an organic relationship of education with the Islamic ethical system. Thus the aim of education was to produce religious and social virtues as enshrined in the Qur'ān and the prophetic traditions. Another aspect of the aim of education was to prepare the child for the performance of religious duties as enjoined by the Qur'ān and the Ḥadīth such as cleaning of body, prayer, fasting, giving of alms (zakāt) and Ḥajj etc.

Besides in Islam science and religion existed side by side. We find many references in the Holy Qur'ān to aspects of natural phenomena exhorting the people to see, to observe and to deduce and to employ nature in the service of mankind. There is great emphasis on attainment of knowledge and learning, hence the attainment of knowledge was also one of the aims of education. In short the goal of Islamic education was to make the individual a true believer in God, his obedient servant and a righteous person and to instil the beliefs and ideals for which Islam stood and to acquire knowledge from wherever available. To another group of Muslims who delved deep into philosophy and science, promotion of rational and scientific outlook in the Muslims was also an important aim of education. This was besides emphasising belief in God and making true Muslims.

Content of Education

Higher Education : The content of higher education varied from group to group as some people emphasised religious sciences while others emphasised philosophy and natural sciences. In the Pre-Ghazzālīan period (excepting the time of the prophet and the pious caliphs) philosophy was given the pride of the place as it was generally believed that there was no clash between philosophy and the tenets of Islam. Plato was considered to be believer in God and Aristotle, a theologian. Many of the Arab philosophers who translated the works of Plato, Aristotle and the neo-Platonists held this view. They included al-Kindī, Ibn Sīnā, al-Fārābī and Ibn Rushd. Thus in the Pre-Ghazzālīan period the courses of studies comprised, Qur'ān, Ḥadīth, Fiqh, Grammar, Arabic literature, Rhetorics, Chemistry, Physics, Astronomy and Mathematics etc.

When al-Ghazzālī appeared on the scene tables were turned against philosophy and rational sciences. He analysed the philosophical concepts of the ancient and the Arab philosophers from the Islamic point of view and refuted most of their ideas and dubbed them as heretical and against the teachings of Islam. His views spread like wild fire among the Muslim scholars of his times and consequently the teaching of philosophy was discouraged and in its place *'Ilm Kalām* (Islamic dialectics) based on the orthodox viewpoint was introduced. Thus philosophy was written of from the list of prescribed subjects in the Madrasas under official patronage. The subjects of studies included, Qur'ān, Ḥadīth, Arabic language, Kalām, elementary astronomy and elementary medicine. This pattern was continued upto the fourteenth century under the patronage of Turk rulers whether in Syria, Egypt, central Asia or India. These rulers were mostly Sunni Muslims and they considered al-Ghazzālī as the saviour of

Islam and the system of education propounded by him as the panacea for all the ills of Muslim society. However, al-Ghazzālī was not totally against secular subjects. He criticised the general tendency in his days of ignoring the study of scientific subjects as well as moral education. He also criticised the sectarian religious education in vogue in his days which resulted in mud slinging on the opposite sects, so he urged that these defects should be rectified.

Elementary Education :—The time for the beginning of education of the child and the subjects to be taught is to found in a Ḥadīth quoted by al-Ghazzālī : "When the child begins to speak he should be taught the *Kalima* i.e. *La Ilāhā īl Allāh.* This should be followed by learning by heart some of the verses of the Qur'ān. The child should be sent to school after attaining the age of seven. In the school he should be taught offering of prayer and writing of passages of the Qur'ān on tablets".[1]

Ibn Sīna suggests the following course for the beginner : "When the boy's limbs become firm and he had attained readiness to speech and is able to assimilate coherent material of language and his ears become perceptive he should begin to receive instruction in the Qur'ān. Letters of alphabet should be drawn for him to copy. He should be taught the precepts of religion. As regards poetry it is desirable that the child should acquire the *Rajaz* poems to begin with and only afterwards *Qasidās*, because recitation of *Rajaz* is easier and its retention in memory more certain as its verses are shorter and matter simpler. The teaching of poetry should come in pieces which contain good morals, praise of science, reproof of ignorance and rebuke of stupidity, which enforces the honouring of parents, practice of good deeds and other noble results.[2]

Methodology :—Methodology of education is closely related to the aims and objectives of education as well as the curriculum. Methodology is in fact the means of achieving the objectives of education as enshrined in the curriculum. The methodology of education should take into consideration the needs, interests, aptitude and inclinations of the pupils and there should be fullest opportunity for the play of intellectual powers. The method adopted for teaching should give ample opportunities for the active participation of the pupils in the teaching learning process instead of merely passive listening. In the Middle Ages we find that the method of teaching emphasised rote learning and passive listening on the part of the pupils. There was little regard for the interests, aptitudes and inclinations of the child. This practice killed the initiative and thinking powers of the pupils and made them dull and docile. In spite of some of these deplorable features of teaching we find that there were some educational theorists like al-Ghazzālī and Ibn Khaldūn who were very critical of this state of affairs and suggested reform of the methodology of education so as to make it psychologically sound and to promote initiative and original thinking in the pupils. They pointed out the need of thorough preparation of the lesson by the teacher because without preparation the teacher cannot do justice to the pupils. They also exhorted the teacher to teach simple things first and then to take up complex things. They should not start teaching complex notions in the beginning. In other words this means that the teacher should have full understanding of the abilities of the pupils. Thus the knowledge imparted in the beginning should be in keeping with the intellectual level of the pupils.

There was no uniform pattern of method of teaching. Each teacher was free to choose his own method. Some teachers emphasised rote learning, others gave an opportunity to the students to study an assignment intelligently and to participate in discussion. However, some of the methods of teaching followed in educational institutions of the Muslims are given below :

1. The text was read by the pupils and its difficulties were explained by the teacher, sometimes the teacher asked the brilliant student to repeat before the teacher what he taught.

2. The teacher delivered a lecture covering some aspects given in the text. Some pupils listened to the lecture and some took notes.

3. One day in every week was devoted to revision so that the teacher may know how far the pupils remember what they

have studied during the week. This method was generally practised in case of younger children.

4. An assignment was given to the pupils for study at home. They were expected to judge, examine and criticise its various aspects such as language, style, diction and thought. This method was meant for advanced students.

5. The teacher allowed discussion on the assignment so as to find out the difficulties of the pupils. This method was also meant for advanced students.

Organisation of Education

The role of teachers : The education system of the Muslims was teacher centred. The teacher held an important place in the whole scheme of things. It was the teacher who determined the plan and execution of the entire education system. Teachers of great learning existed before the colleges came into existence. They taught at their houses or in a corner of a mosque. After the establishment of colleges when the number of students increased the teacher was helped by a number of assistants (*Mu'īd*) whose duty was to repeat the lesson before the class for elucidation of difficulties. They were appointed from among the brighter students. The *Mu'id* sometimes officiated in the absence of the teacher. The teachers were regular in their work and demanded rigourously the same from the pupils. They appeared in proper dress which was a turban and a long flowing garment which was the hallmark of the scholarly class.

The status of teachers : The teachers were expected to maintain a reserved and dignified behaviour and to adhere to it with most scrupulous care in public because they had to maintain the dignity of knowledge and the learned profession. The teacher's status and prestige was measured by the size of assembly which gathered to listen to his lecture and also by the number of distinguished scholars which had graduated under him. The teachers were often appointed as ambassadors and ministers because of their eloquence and scholarship. *e.g.* Sheikh Abū Ishāq the first principal of Nizamia Madrasa in Baghdad was sent by Abbasid Caliph to Sultān Malik Shāh at Nishāpūr as an ambassador.[3]

Appointment of teachers : During the early period when education was not institutionalised the appointment of the teachers was made by the senior teacher on the basis of his suitability for the job and his reputation among the students and his successful career as Mu'īd. Many important scholars were appointed in this way. Imām Ghazzālī was nominated for the post of teaching by his teacher Imām al-Ḥarmain.

Later on when the education system developed and large number of Madrasas were founded by philanthropists and princes the appointment of the teachers was made by the Mutawallī (manager) or the patron of the Madrasa.

Salaries of teachers : In the state owned institutions of higher learning the teachers were given allowances similar to those given to savants. Sometimes the salaries of the teachers were given from the endowments made by princes and other philanthropists. Sometime aid was given from the public exchequer. Nizāmul Mulk earmarked 700,000 dirhams annually from the public exchequer for the Niẓamia Madrasa. In addition to this an equal amount of grant was given from his privy purse. According to Ibn-Jubbair Sultan Salaḥuddīn defrayed the entire expenses of the Madrassa at Cairo, amounting to about 2,000 Egyptian dinars per mensum.[4] In Damascus the salaries of the teachers amounted to 30,000 dinars annually which was paid from the public treasury.[5]

Boarding and Lodging : In the early period there was no organised system for providing board and lodging to the pupils and they had to face a lot of difficulty in making the arrangement for their stay for getting the benefit of higher education. But when an organised system of Madrasa education came into existence the provision for board and lodging was made for students coming from far off places on account of the fame of the institutions and its teachers. By the time prosperous and independent states were founded a large number of Madrasas were established with the support of the rulers and the nobility provision was made for the board and lodging of the students. In those days students hostels formed part of composite plan which included a mosque, a mausoleum and the Madrasa. The students living in the hostel had to follow rules and regulations of the hostels and to show examplary standard of morality and culture as expected from members of the learned profession.

Library : Today the library is considered an essential part of a teaching institution. So it was in the Islamic world in the Middle Ages. In the hey day of Islamic empire good libraries were established by the rulers at Baghdad and Cairo. With these libraries were attached Academies and translation bureaus. Later on when Madrasas were established, the libraries formed an essential part of these Madrasas. The Nizamia Madrasa at Baghdad had a rich library attached to it. The rulers and nobles gifted their own valuable treasure of books to the library. The management of the library was entrusted to scholars of repute. In addition to libraries attached to the Madrasas there were public libraries in big towns.

Examination and degrees : In the Islamic world, in those days there was no formal examination for awarding degrees. The assessment of the attainment of the pupils was made by teacher concerned. In some cases the pupil had to undergo a public test in the form of a debate or a lecture. At the end of the course the student was given a certificate of permission to teach (Ijāza). The students who completed their education were vested with academic gown and the certificate.

References

1. Goldziher : *Encyclopaedia of Religion and Ethics*, Article under Education (Muslim), Vol. V, p. 206, quoted from Ibn Sīna : *Risāla al-Siyāsa*.
2. *Ibid*.
3. Abdul Ghafoor : *Some Aspects of Islamic Education*, Lahore 1951, p. 9.
4. *Ibid.*
5. *Ibid*., p. 83.

Chapter IX

CONCLUSION

Resume : Characteristic features of Muslim Education

The distinguishing feature of Islamic education is the place it gives to the Holy Qur'ān which is the word of God revealed to Prophet Moḥammad (Peace be on him), as guidance to mankind. The Muslims thought it proper to base their education on the Qur'ān so that the successive generations may get perennial and continuous guidance. The Qur'ān contains the fundamental tenets of Islam and the rules and regulations governing the life of the Muslims. The Qur'ān is the source of Islamic law and the social and economic organisation. It is also because of the sanctity of the Qur'ān, that it has been given the pride of the place in curriculum of the child as well as the adult. The second position has been given to the traditions (Ḥadīth) which contains the sayings of the Prophet on religious matters as well as day to day problems of the Muslims. Ḥadīth deals with all the aspects of the life of the Muslims as how to offer prayer, how to deal with brothers, neighbours, friends and foes etc. At the elementary level the traditions of moral and ethical significance are taught and at the advanced level principles of Ḥadīth and principles of Fiqh (jurisprudence) are taught. Arabic language is also compulsory because it is the language of the Qur'ān. Language at the advanced level includes grammar, syntax and literature. Philosophy and astronomy are also taught.

Education under the early Abbasids was characterised by eclecticism and spirit of enquiry with scant respect to fundamental beliefs of religion. The rulers patronised learned men such as the philosophers and the Mu'tazila and established institutions of higher learning and research. However, the cultivation of science and philosophy was marred by repression against those who did not toe the official line as they did not like interference in matters of faith, *e.g.* the Mu'tazila believed that the Qur'ān was created and it was not eternal. Such views were objected to by the theologians but al-Ma'mūn and his immediate successors tried to compel the theologians to accept the views of Mu'tazila but they refused to oblige, so al-Ma'mūn and some of his successors unleashed a reign of terror against the theologians and threw them into prison and tormented them but their faith was unshaken.

The later Abbasid caliph reversed the policies of al-Ma'mūn and his immediate successors and ended the persecution of the 'Ulema on the one hand and curbed the free thought of the Mu'tazila on the other. They were as harsh on them as al-Ma'mūn was in relation to 'Ulema. Thus the balance tilted in favour of orthodoxy and greater emphasis was laid on Islamic sciences such as Qur'ān, Ḥadīth and Fiqh etc. With the weakening of the central authority of the Abbasid caliph many principalities and ruling dynasties sprang up such as the Buwehids of Persia, the Samanids of Bukhara and the Fatimids of Egypt. The Buwehids supported Shiite doctrines and gave refuge to Mu'tazila. The Fatimids propagated the doctrines of Isma'ilism and supported free thought. The Seljūq ruler Malik Shah (Xth century) who was a Sunni reoriented the education system according to Sunni ideology. He took the help of al-Ghazzālī and Nizamul Mulk (his vazier) in his respect. Al-Ghazzālī introduced a new philosophy of education emphasising the religious and ethical aspect. This was in marked contrast to the study of philosophy and sciences during the reigns of early Abbasids. Al-Ghazzālī fought the philosophers, the Mutazilites and the Fatimid ideology at the intellectual plane and cleared and purified Islam of all sort of heresies and un-Islamic doctrines which had infiltrated into Islam during the preceding period. In the Ghazzālīan system of education the Qur'ān, Ḥadīth and Fiqh were given priority and philosophy and sciences were neglected. This system continued for about 200 years when some of the defects of the prevailing education system were pointed out by Ibn Khaldūn, although he himself accepted the broad features of the system.

Impact of Muslim Educational Thought on West

The greatest intellectual movement of Medieval Europe was scholasticism which influenced learning in those days. The aim of the movement was to prove the religious tenets by reason. This was a great advance in their approach towards religion, as in the preceding centuries the acceptance of the doctrines of Christianity was essential and nobody could question them. The European scholars got the idea of scholasticism from a similar science popular in the lands of Islam. The science was called 'Ilm Kalām which applied the principles of logic and philosophy for the explanation of the tenets of Islam. This science appealed to the European religious leaders and scholars who were faced with the problem of skepticism. Some of the greatest scholars of Medieval Europe were champions of scholasticim such as Albert Magnus and Thomas Acquinas. These and many other scolars in addition to writing voluminous works on scholastic interpretation of Christian doctrines were credited to have translated the works of Muslim philosophers of Spain such as Ibn Rushd as well as al-Ghazzālī and al-Kindī etc. In this respect the Arab philosophers of Spain played a leading role. About the influence of Spanish philosopher Hitti says : "The crowning achievement of the intellectual class of the Arab and Spain was in the realm of philosophical thought. Here they formed the last and the strongest link which transmitted Greek philosophy as transmitted by them and their eastern co-religionists to Latin west adding their own contribution in reconciling faith, reason, religion and science. . . . . This marks the beginning of the end of Dark Ages and the dawn of scholastic period kindled by contact with Arab thought."[1]

Another influence of the philosophical and educational thought of the Muslims on Europe is to be found in the origin of the universities in the eleventh and twelfth century Europe. The Europeans knew that universities and centres of religious learning existed in different parts of the empire of Islam such as in Baghdad, Cairo and Nisabur in the east and the universities of Cordova, Seville, Malaqa and Granada in the west. These centres of learning were primarily centres of religious learning but where other subjects were also taught. In Europe in those days there were great centres of religious learning at Paris and Oxford. Later on these centres of learning were turned into universities encompassing all the important sciences, arts and philosophy. In this way it can be said that the foundation of universities in Europe got the inspiration for expanding the scope of learning from the education system prevailing in the Islamic countries. In this respect the universities of Cordova and Seville might have influenced the European centres of religious learning to a greater extent than of Baghdad and Cairo because of proximity to Europe and also because of the fact that many European scholars went to Spain for study in the Universities of Cordova and Seville.

A critical examination of the education system of the Muslims

1. *The Muslim education system failed to achieve universalisation of education* : In spite of the fact that the Qur'ān made acquisition of knowledge obligatory for all Muslims, men and women and some states patronised learning and established schools and academies, education was by and large a personal affair. It depended to a large extent on individual rulers interested in education who patronised scholars and established educational institutions. Teaching was generally done by scholars at their homes or in mosques. Only those people joined the courses of studies who were interested in education for its own sake. Universalisation of education as stipulated in Islam was a far cry.

2. *Florescence of the Golden Age of Islam lost* : It is well known that during the 8th and 9th centuries great were strides taken in all the fields of learning. Greek works translated were into Arabic and Persian and original works were written on philosophy and sciences and centres of learning and research were established in Baghdad and other important cities of the Islamic empire. By the end of the 9th century the conditions changed because of the weakening of the central authority and the religious fanaticism of the faction ridden Muslim society. There were some efforts on the part of the newly formed states

by establishing centres of learning in Cairo, Baghdad and Shiraz but these institutions were concerned with factional and sectarian ideologies and were engrossed in religious squabbles.

Some Misconceptions about Muslim Education Dispelled

1. *Al-Ghazzālī was responsible for the decay of sciences* : Some Orientalists are of the view that al-Ghazzālī with his retrograde ideas which finds expression in the education system introduced by him was responsible for the decay of sciences. Sarton, however, refutes this charge in these words : "Al-Ghazzālī was too noble and broad minded intellectual to be accused of obscurantism and at any rate no man, however, could stop the natural growth of national genious.[2] This clearly shows that to hold al-Ghazzālī responsible for the decline of sciences is a lop-sided view and ignores other contributary factors such as political instability and the multiplicity of sects and creeds. The followers of these sects and creeds were always at logger-heads. Thus lack of political stability and persecution of scholars for not subscribing to the views of the rulers was in fact responsible for the decay of sciences. The conditions were so chaotic that hordes or people were on the move from their hearth and home in search of peace and security. This condition prevailed for centuries. Scholars were particular targets of oppression. In spite of these inhospitable condition we come accross many scholars who wrote monumental works. But such scholars were few and far between.

It will be of interest to point out the views of Ibn Khaldūn[3] on the subject of decay of sciences among the Muslims. He pointed out that in the beginning Islam had no science or craft. This was due to the simple conditions of desert life. These people did not know anything about scientific instruction or writing of books or systematic works. There was no incentive for that. By the time of the reign of al-Rashid it was found necessary to write commentaries on the Qur'ān and to preserve the traditions in writing. In the meantime the Arabic language became corrupt so arose the need to lay down the rules of grammar. The laws and norms of religious sciences were formulated by analogical reasoning. Other auxiliary sciences became necessary such as the rules of Arabic language and books on defence of articles of faith by argument because of rampant heresies and innovations. The sciences were cultivated by sedentary people who were at that time non-Arabs *i.e.* the Persians who were experts in sciences since the time of the Persian empire. The Arabs who came into contact with that flourishing sedentary people changed the Beduin attitude yet they still tried to shun scholarship because of their pre-occupation with government. They considered it to be a contemptible thing to be a scholar because scholarship was considered a craft. Thus non-Arabs and the Persians continued to occupy position of eminence. This situation continued in all the important cities as long as Persia and the Persian countries such as 'Irāq, Khurāsān and Transoxiana retained their sedentary culture but when these countries fell into ruin sedentary culture disappeared from them. But soon Cairo became the seat of sedentary culture which was marked by cultivation of sciences. Here are the words of Ibn Khaldūn: "Today (late 14th century) no city has more sedentary culture than Cairo. It is the mother of world and the great centre of Islam and the mainspring of science and craft."[4]

2. *Muslim Education was purely religious* : This is also a distorted view of Muslim education. A perusal of the courses of studies discussed in this book will prove to the contrary. There was not a single Madrasa worth the name where only religious education was imparted. The courses included besides religious sciences, philosophy, literature, medicine and astronomy. If we examine closely the views of some of the educationists like Ibn Sīnā, al-Ghazzālī and Ibn Khaldūn we will find that they pleaded for the study of sciences and philosophy. Ibn Sīnā emphasised the need of training the students in arts and crafts so that a child after finishing his education may devote himself to some craft for earning his living. In Islamic society work by hand was not despised. There are examples of scholars who earned their living through some vocation and devoted their spare time to studies. They pursued their education for knowledge and not for getting employment

as is the case nowadays. They led an austere life, had no greed for worldly riches and cared more for the world to come rather than this transitory and perishable world.

3. *Muslim education encouraged fundamentalism* : Islamic education emphasised fundamentalism in the sense that it could not tolerate interference in the fundamental tenets of Islam by skeptics and innovators who wanted to distort Islam by changing its fundamental to suit their whims. So the Muslims in following their religion as enshrined in the Qur'ān and the Ḥadīth cannot be called fundamentalists in the sense the word is nowadays used *i.e.* a rabid form of communalism and factionalism responsible for instigating ill-will among various groups. Religion is a matter of faith so any one professing a certain religion must follow it in letter and spirit by accepting its fundamentals and following them scrupulously. So, in Islamic education the pride of the place was given to making the Muslim true Muslims by following the Qur'ān and the Ḥadīth in all matters religious or secular and not for bartering their faith with worldly benefits.

4. *Muslim education was responsible for backwardness of Muslim society* : This also is a prejudiced view. Education in those days was not such an important force as to be held responsible for the backwardness of the masses. Even today edncation is dependent on other forces such as state, techniques and values etc. According to Ottaway : education is no doubt an important means of bringing about change in the society but it is subordinate to other social forces such as state, religion, techniques and values.[6] Of this lot the state is the most important of all. It holds the key to the type of education it wants to impart. It determines the whole system of education. A totalitarian state will subordinate the individual to the needs of the society and the welfare of the state. A democratic state will give greater freedom to the people but will have its say in determining the aim and content of education. In the Middle Ages the states were neither totalitarian nor democratic. There were monarchies. The rulers were more concerned with consolidation of their empire rather the welfare of the people. Consequently education was generally neglected. There were few exceptions. Education

in those days was looked after by philanthropists and scholars. In these conditions how can the Muslim education be considered such a strong force as to be held responsible for the backwardness of the society. In fact it was the duty of the state to take steps for the amelioration of the people but the state shirked its responsibility.

Relevance of Muslim educational thought today

Generally speaking Muslim educational thought laid great stress on the religious and spiritual aspect but at the same time it did not ignore the study of secular and rational sciences. An important feature of the education system of the Muslims as gleaned from the ideas of Muslim educationists is that in addition to moral and religious education they emphasised the need of imparting instruction in arts and crafts so that after finishing their education they may earn their living. A Muslim scholar was not ashamed of working by hand for earning his living. Thus it may be said the education system of the Muslims was oriented towards self employment and at no stage was responsible for unemployment among the educated people. The stress on religious and spiritual aspect is all the more important in the world of today as religion has been completely driven away from the school because of the emphasis on material progress at the expense of the moral and spiritual aspect of man. Its results are before us in the form of complete neglect of moral and ethical values. This is the situation not only in the developed countries like Europe and America but in the developing countries of the third world. The developed countries because of certain favourable factors such as the exploitation of the natural resources of the down-trodden people in the colonial period which preceded the present industrialisation period, reaped the full harvest of material progress by sacrificing religious and moral education, but the developing countries in imitating the west lost both. The new generation that has come up in these countries is ignorant of their cultural heritage and the moral and social values. The people are so much enamoured by material progress that money has become all important and is to be earned by all means. Corruption is rampant in all walks of life. The situation can only be improved if ethical and moral values are emphasised in the schools.

Lastly the relevance of Muslim educational thought lies in the fact that it can imbibe in the Muslims the ideals for which Islam stands. However, some changes in the system of education are needed such as introduction of instruction in modern subjects such as natural sciences, social sciences etc. so that side by side getting the benefit of Islamic education the student may opt for advanced studies in engineering, medicine, business and other vocations open to other students.

References

1. Hitti : *History of the Arabs*, p. 580.
2. Sarton : *Introduction to the History of Science*, Vol. I, p. 747.
3. Ibn Khaldūn: *Muqaddima* (Prolegomena), Translation by Rosenthal, Vol. III, p. 310-15.
4. *Ibid.*, p. 316.
5. *Supra* : Views of Ibn Sīna, al-Ghazzālī, Ibn Khaldūn.
6. Ottaway : *Education and Society*, London, pp. 12, 52.

APPENDIX A

MUSLIM EDUCATION IN INDIA—HISTORICAL PERSPECTIVE

Muslim education in India right from the first Muslim ruler to the last Mughal king has undergone many changes and modifications. The contribution made by various Muslim rulers towards the promotion of education has been analysed here. Further, the crisis faced by Muslim education during the British rule has also been discussed along with various steps taken by the Britishers to improve the condition of Muslim education. The partition of the country, again caused a serious backlash to the Muslim education in India and from this emerged the momentum for the existing Muslim education movement. The treatment meted out to the Muslim education in the post-independence era has also been discussed in the light of the minority's concern towards their identity and rights.

I. Social Status of the Teacher

The teacher occupied the highest position in the Islamic society. Teaching and imparting of knowledge has been considered to be the noblest occupation and the teacher enjoyed a place of honour and respect. Learning and scholarship were the virtues prized most in the Islamic society and a Muslim considered imparting of education a meritorious deed and would do his best to carry forward the torch of knowledge. In India during the Muslim era the learned were loved and respected all over the country. The state also encouraged them in all possible ways.

The teachers were very proud of their occupation. They would never do anything which might reflect badly on their character and profession. Their character was crystal clear and their integrity was absolutely unshakable. They commanded universal respect and confidence, though their emoluments were small. The spiritual force of their character could not be doubted and the efficiency of their teaching was never called in question.

The teacher loved his students and there existed very affectionable relationship between them. The students had constant intellectual communion with the teacher. The present system of commercialisation of education was unknown. No regular fee was charged from the students and sometimes they were provided with free board and lodging by the teachers.

The teachers and students enjoyed freedom of thought and expression and they were encouraged to promote their noble profession. Consequently, it was only within first few centuries of the advent of Islam, that the Muslim scholarship of highest order developed in all the Islamic countries both in traditional and intellectual sciences. This was true of India also.

The *modus operandi* of imparting education usually consisted of religious discourses and teaching in mosques. However, with the new facets of teaching the concept of Madrasa emerged, which were usually located in or around the premises of the mosque. But over the centuries the mosques more or less retained the character of Madrasa in the different parts of the Islamic world.

II. The role of Madrasas

The Madrasas were most important institutions of Islamic civilisation. Ziayuddin has pointed out that Madrasas were open to every interested person, with the result that learning was widespread among all the types of people and groups. The curriculum was mainly centred upon the Qur'ān, but subjects like Grammar, stories of prophets and elementary principles of Arithmetic were also taught. The prevalent system of imparting instruction was lecture. The debates and seminars were also held and issues pertaining to a problem were discussed in detail. The Madrasas played very important role in the economic and educational uplift of the Muslims. Its religious, educational, political and social significance far over-shadowed that of other institutions. It trained religious and government officials, served as a hostel for merchants, pilgrims and travellers. It was the site for legal courts, provided business opportunities, employment and contributed to the creation and integration of Islamic society.

In India during the Muslim period educational institutions were not divided into religious and secular. There was only one type of school called Madrasas, where both religious and secular subjects were taught. Jaffar has stated that mosques and Monasteries (Khanqahs) which were founded and endowed throughout Muslim India became a valuable asset to education in general. Their importance as centres of both spiritual and secular learning cannot be under estimated, as they were often availed of by scholars for the recitation of their books. They were also used for lecture halls and schools. Almost every mosque of importance had a school and a library attached to it. They played an important role in the dissemination of knowledge, both religious and general.

In the beginning of the nineteenth century, the non-Madrasas type of schools began to appear throughout the country. These schools which were run and aided by the Christian missions made their headway in a very short span of time. On the other hand the Madrasas retained their importance till the beginning of the second half of the century, because Madrasa graduates were also considered to be qualified for the government service. But with gradual change in state policy towards Muslim education it was almost impossible for a Madrasa graduate to find an important position in the government service. Further, the Government established and patronised the modern schools and colleges for secular education and showed no inclination to support the then existing Muslim educational system.

The Muslims, however, stuck to Madrasa education to preserve their identity and culture. In 1865, a Madrasa now known as Darul Ulum was started at Deoband and a scheme was developed to start a network of Madrasas all over northern India. The starting of Deoband spurred the Muslim community to open Madrasas in different towns to provide their children with religious education.

Darul-Ulum, Deoband was initially housed in a mosque and later shifted to a rented house. It has its first independent building in 1879 and thereafter gradually a number of buildings and halls for different departments and Faculties were added. At present Darul-Ulum enjoys international character.

One of the main objective of Darul-Ulum was to provide the Indian Muslims with a direct access to the original sources of Islamic learning, produce learned men with missionary zeal to work in their own community. The institution has achieved this objective to a great extent and has produce a large number of outstanding religious leaders and learned men most of them have made valuable contributions in different branches of Islamic learning. It has been rightly pointed out that a Madrasa at Deoband established itself as a school of religious thought and a large number of Madrasas were founded on its lines throughout the country by those who graduated from it, thus bringing religious education to a large section of the Muslims.

The Darul-Ulum's curriculum was purely religious in nature, therefore, soon after its establishment the Ulema began to realise that the Madrasa curriculum was inadequate for modern times. Further, with the introduction of University education in India, it was also felt that the two educational systems were creating division among educated Muslims. To bridge the gap, various attempts were made to revise the Madrasa curriculum to accommodate the merits of modern education without losing its religious character.

In 1892 Majlis-i-Nadwatul Ulema was formed and two years later a Madrasa, Darul-Ulum Nadwatul Ulema was founded in Lucknow. This institution also faced many difficulties in introducing along with the religious, the secular education. A salient feature of this institution is its emphasis of independent research. A dissertation or thesis on any general subject is obligatory for the post-graduate students.

The movement for the secular education for the Muslims gained momentum and modern educational institutions were established. The most important of these being Aligarh

Muslim University, Aligarh and Jamia Millia Islamia, New Delhi.

The founder of Aligarh Muslim University Sir Syed Ahmad Khan was of the view that the backwardness of the Muslim community was due to their neglect of modern education. He, therefore, conceived the idea of imparting modern education to Muslims in literature and science while at the same time instruction was to be given in Muslim religion and tradition also. With this objective in mind he constituted a committee to devise ways and means for educational regeneration of Muslims. In consequence of the activities of the Committee, a school was established in May 1873 which took the shape of a High School. In 1877, Lord Lytton, the then Viceroy of India, laid the foundation stone of Mohammadan Anglo-Oriental College. This College attracted a considerable number of students and finally in the year 1920, the College emerged as a University. At present besides various Faculties and Departments, the University has a Department of Islamic Studies and Theology which almost cover the whole range of Islamic learning. The Institut e of Islamic Studies was also established in the University in the year 1954 to promote the study of Islamic Culture and Civilisation.

Jamia Millia Islamia, New Delhi came into existence through the effects of Muslim stalwarts like Maulana Mohammad Ali, Dr. Mukhtar Ahmad Ansari, Hakim Ajmal Khan and Dr. Zakir Hussain. The foundation stone of Jamia Millia was laid by Shaikhul Hind Maulana Mahmudul Hasan, Principal of Dural Ulum Deoband. The Jamia Millia was established in 1920 at Aligarh from where it was shifted to Delhi. The Jamia which was intended to be an Islamic National Educational Institution imparted instruction in modern subjects along with religious instruction independent from the official system and control. After independence the Jamia attained the status of a university with a number of Departments of Studies. It also maintains a Department of Islamic Studies. There are various other institutions and centres of learning where education is imparted and research projects undertaken. No doubt, various educational institutions were established for the promotion of Muslim education in India, but the development of

Muslim education in itself has a long history which has been discussed briefly in the following pages.

III. The Development of Muslim Education

With the coming of the Muslims in India education got a new impetus and almost all the rulers made their contribution to the cause of education particularly of the Muslims. The development of Muslim education can well be described in four stages or period *i.e.* the pre-Mughal period. The Mughal period, the British period and the post-independence period.

(i) *The pre-Mughal period* : A reference to growth and development of Muslim education in this period is to be found in Chapter I, pages 6-9.

(ii) *The Mughal period* : The Mughals unfolded a new chapter in the history of Muslim education. Babar the founder of the dynasty was himself a great scholar. He gave due attention for the promotion of education and many educational institutions were constructed in his regime of four years. Nasir-ud-din Muhammad Humayun, successor of Babar did his best to promote education. He conferred a special status to the teachers and scholars. Humayun ruled India for a continuous period of ten years and thereby succeeded in introducing considerable changes in the existing pattern of education. He was deposed by the Shor Shah Suri of Suri Dynasty. In a span of four years Sher Shah also promoted the educational policy and established various Madrasas, the famous of them being Sher Shahi Madrasa. His successors were not good administrators. Humayun took the advantage of such state of affairs and conquered the throne of Delhi again in 1553 A.D.

Humayun's son Akbar was equally interested in the promotion of education. He, for the promotion of higher education, established Colleges at Agra, Fatehpur Sikri, Lahore, Delhi and other important towns in his empire. He sanctioned liberal grants to the educational institutions. He established a big library at Agra which contained as many as 24,000 books. As a result of prevailing prosperity and peace a rich quality of literature was established in the Akbar's regime. Faizi and Abul Fazal were some of the Persian scholars who enriched every branch of the persian literature. His reign was also golden age of Hindi poetry. The most famous luminaries of Hindi literature were Tulsi Das, Sur Das, Ras Khan, Keshav Das and others. It was no doubt Sikandar Lodi who made Agra an important centre of education but Babar and Humayun also contributed towards this mission and established various Madrasas at Agra. Further, it was Akbar who made Agra not only a Centre of learning but also a seat of Culture, Crafts and Fine Arts. During the regime of Akbar, Agra emerged in the shape of a big University town and attracted scholars from various parts of the world.

In Akbar's period Lahore was also an eminent centre of learning. Akbar introduced many reforms in the system of education and the curriculum was so modified as to enable the students as to acquire education according to their aims and ambitions. The ideals and objectives of education were changed from being strictly religious to secular. Akbar aimed at imparting of education to all classes of his subjects irrespective of their race, religion, caste or creed. After him Jahangir, Shah Jahan and Aurangzeb also showed keen interest in the promotion of education.

(iii) *Muslim Education in the British Period* : Some historians are of the view that the system of education at the time of the Muslim rulers was not satisfactory. Such a view is not based on facts and is quite far away from the truth. As pointed out in the preceding pages the Muslim rulers introduced many changes in the educational set up and considerable advance was made towards providing better facilities and opportunities to the people for pursuing their studies. According to Sir Monro the education system of Muslim India was better than that of many European countries of the time, though inferior to the English system.

The British rulers were interested in changing the pattern of education to suit their needs as the then existing system of education was not satisfactory for them. The Muslim masses did not like the British system of education. They were particularly averse to learning the English language. This harmed the Muslims and weakened their position and they gradually began to lose all important offices. The abolition of Muslim

Criminal Law and the introduction of Indian Penal Code deprived the Muslims from appointment in the legal profession.

The Muslim education system went on decline and it got a serious set back in 1865, when orders were issued that examinations for all important positions shall be held in English only. The Muslims remained aloof from the British educational system and thus got themselves deprived from its advantages. The Muslim education continued to suffer and the Muslims were out-numbered in almost every field.

The sorry state of affairs of Muslim education proved an eye opener for the Muslim social reformers who showed keen interest in improving the condition of Muslim education. Sir Syed Ahmad Khan took lead in this venture and in the year 1863 he established the Scientific Society at Ghazipur[1] with the object of stimulating Muslims to go in for modern education. The Scientific Society took the shape of Aligarh Movement and finally emerged in the shape of Aligarh Muslim University. Sir Syed Ahmad pointed out that the main objective of this movement was to motivate the Muslims to secure modern education.[2] Various other institutions were also established for this purpose.

The Britishers were fully conscious that education was essential for the consolidation of their rule in India. They appointed various commissions to look into the system of education and to recommend measures thereof. The Hunter Commission of which Justice Syed Mahmud was also a member, presented a very depressing picture of education among the Muslims. The educational backwardness among Indian Muslims made Earl Mayo to observe :

"It is much to be regretted that so large and important a class, possessing a classical literature replete with the works of profound learning and knowledge, should stand alone from active cooperation with our educational system and should lose the advantage, both material and social which others enjoys."[3]

The British government in India directed the provincial Governments to encourage classical and vernacular languages of Muslims in all Government schools and colleges and to appoint Muslim teachers in all the Muslim populated areas. Further the Provincial Governments were asked to provide 'grant in aid' to the Muslim communities to enable them to establish schools of their own. It was also suggested that a special section be devoted to Muslim education in the Annual Reports of Public Institutions, so as to keep the Government of India informed about the progress of education among the Muslims. Scholarships were provided to the Muslims for higher education. The policy attracted the Muslims towards English system of education.

The Reports of the Provincial Governments were reviewed at length by the Education Commission of 1882. It laid much emphasis on the promotion of education among the Muslims and after detailed debates and discussions recommended the following proposals :[4]

(i) Indigenous schools for the Muslims should be liberally encouraged to add secular subjects to their curriculum.
(ii) In the Public Primary Schools for Muslims, special standard should be prescribed.
(iii) Higher English Education for Muslims both in Schools and Colleges should be encouraged.
(iv) Scholarship at all levels should be made available to Muslim students.
(v) The benefits of the Muslim Educational Endowments should be reserved for the Muslim students to promote their education.
(vi) Special provisions should be made to increase the number of Muslim teachers and other officers.
(vii) Employment should be offered to the Muslims in Public Offices by Local Governments.

The recommendations of the Commission were carried out by the Government in spite of the fact that such recommendations were criticised on many counts by other communities. This policy of the Government showed good results. The number of Muslim students increased from 114,816 in 1871-72 to 261,887 in 1881-82. The educational progress in the four years following the Commission's report showed that the number and percentage of the students attending the schools went up considerably, but there was no improvement at higher level. From 1886 to 1897, the total number of the Muslim students increased from 754,036 to 966,632, but generally speaking the Muslim education did not advance beyond the primary stage.[5] The steady efforts made by the Government to ameliorate their lot as well as to change the attitude of the leaders of their community towards education more favourable.[6] But progress made by the Muslims in the field of education particularly in the technical education was not satisfactory.

The Government continued with its efforts to improve the education system in the country. The percentage of illiteracy in the total population steadily decreased from 93.8 in 1901 to 90.9 in 1931. In the same year there were near about 219 million persons of 10 years and above age, who could neither read nor write. They constituted 90.9 per cent of the total population at that age level. However, figures refer to pre-partition India including Pakistan and Bangladesh.[7] Literacy in English in the same group increased from 0.5 per cent in 1901 to 1.4 per cent in 1931. The position of the Muslims in the English education was worst. The 1941 census also showed that illiteracy was considerably reduced but increasing population added new dimensions to illiteracy.

(iv) *Muslim Education and Independent India*

In the year 1947 *i.e.* at the time of independence India started with a very low level of literacy. In 1951 the literacy rate in the population aged 10 and over was 29.6 per cent for males and 9.4 per cent for females. Such low rates of literacy have not been observed in any of the so-called developed countries during their recorded history. The Muslims continued to be lagging behind in the field of education, in spite of all the steps taken by the British Government to improve their lot.

The Independent India felt the great need of expansion of education at all stages particularly at the stage of primary education. The National leaders like Mahatma Gandhi, Pt.

Jawahar Lal Nehru, Abul Kalam Azad and other stalwarts were fully conscious of the fact that very soul of the democratic country is education. Literacy and education are essential conditions for national development. Further, national stalwarts firmly believed that education of the masses is essential for the smooth functioning of the democratic country. The framers of the Indian Constitution keeping in view the importance of education made necessary provisions for its promotion. The constitution of India, accordingly directs the state Governments to provide free and compulsory education to all children upto the age of 14 years. All states have made primary education free but only a few states have taken steps towards compulsory education.

Education in India being a state subject, therefore, the entire responsibility for its promotion is primarily on the state Government. However, the centre provides some facilities and plays the role of an advisory body. It provides funds and experts opinion for the expansion of education. The centres also formulates All India policies in education. A number of commissions have been appointed to look into the system of education and suggest measures for its improvement. The first Indian Education Commission known as Radha Krishan Commission was appointed in the year 1948. It was followed by Secondary Education Commission or Mudaliar Commission in 1953 and National Commission (Kothari Commission, 1964-66). A number of Committees were also appointed from time to time and the education policy was reviewed after every five years. A drastic change in the Education Policy has been introduced by the Constitutional Amendment of 1976, wherein the education has been included in the concurrent list. The role and responsibility of the states in regard to the education will remain essentially unchanged, but large responsibility is now on the Union Government to promote the education at the national level.

The Muslim education suffered a serious set-back in the year 1947, when the country was divided on the basis of religion. Pakistan, no doubt emerged as a separate nation, but the Muslims continue to be the largest minority in the country. The National Commissions and Committees made various recommendations for universalization of the elementary education, but they failed to pay any special attention towards the education of the Muslims—the most educationally backward class.

The strength of the Muslims in the educational institutions continue to be at very low ebb even after four decades of independence. The enrolment of the Muslim boys and girls is comparatively very low even in the Muslim managed schools. An all India survey of 430 Muslim managed schools and 44 Muslim managed colleges, conducted by the Hamdard Educational Society, showed that the percentage of non-Muslim students in such schools keep on increasing as the level of education rises from lower to higher level.[8] Further, the survey of the examination results of the class X and class XII conducted by the Central Board of the Secondary Education from 1978 to 1983 showed that there was no Muslim name in the list of first seventy successful students.[9] Further, in 1980, 25307 students from various colleges of the Delhi University, appeared to get bachelor's degree, out of which only 1.47 per cent were Muslims. In B. Com., B. Sc. and Engineering, their ratio was 1.05, 1.30 and 1.04 respectively.[10] The percentage of the Muslims in various government and semi-government institutions and departments is very low and in some offices their percentage is insignificant. It is rather an accepted fact that representation of minority communities in the government services, industries, banks and other organisations is very low. This clearly shows that the educational backwardness of the Muslims has continued to be on the same footing as it was in the pre-partition days.

The minority educational institutions continued to be the back-bone of the Muslim education in India. In the pre-independence era various steps were taken by the Government of India to boost and promote education of the Muslims. In the post-independence period various Commissions and Committees were appointed from time to time, to suggest measures for improvement of the education system in the country. But such Commissions and Committees failed to pay any special attention towards education of the Muslims, consequently the educational backwardness among Muslims increased with the increase in their population. However, the framers of the constitution were alive of the problems of minority education and they, therefore, provided constitutional safeguards for the minority educational institutions. The constitution of India in this respect provides :

1. Art. 30(1). All minorities whether based on religion or language shall have the right to establish and administer educational institutions of their choice.

2. The State shall not, in granting aid to the educational institutions discriminate against any educational institution on the ground that it is under the management of a minority whether based on religion or language.

Further, Art. 350A, provides that it shall be the endeavour of every state and of every local authority within the state to provide adequate facilities for instruction in the mother-tongue at the primary stage of education to children belonging to the linguistic minority groups and the President may issue such directions to the state as he considers necessary and proper for securing the provisions of such facilities.

The Supreme Court of India[11] has pointed out that the right provided under Art. 30(1) is a fundamental right declared in terms absolute. It is intended to be a real right for the protection of the minorities in the matter of setting up of educational institutions of their choice. The right is intended to be effective and is not to be whittled down by so-called regulatory measures conceived in the interest not of the minority educational institutions, but of the public or nation as a whole. The court further observed that, if every order which while maintaining the formal character of a minority institution destroys the power of administration is held justifiable because it is in the public or national interest, though not in its interest as an educational institution, the right guaranteed by Art. 30(1) will be but a 'teasing illusion', a promise of unreality. Regulations which may lawfully be imposed either by legislative or executive action as a condition of receiving grant or of recognition must be directed to making the institution while retaining its character as a minority institution. Such regulation must satisfy a dual test—the test of reasonableness and the test that it is regulative of the educational character of the institution and is conducive to making the institution an effective vehicle of education for the minority community or other persons who resort to it.

The guarantee contained under Articles 20 and 30 is a part of the pledge to secure justice, liberty and equality, expressed so solemnly in the preamble and is a part of the ideal so demonstrably ingrained throughout the constitution which aims at establishment of a welfare state and a national social order in which inequalities, discrimination and arbitrariness are sought to be levelled down to the minimum. The object of these provisions is to protect religious and linguistic minorities from discrimination and to allow them to preserve their linguistic and cultural characteristics. Educational institutions being one of the most effective methods preservation of such characteristics, what the constitution seeks to secure to these minorities is a right to establish and administer educational institutions on their own choice and preferment.

The constitutional safeguards are indeed a reaffirmation of the faith that India shall be just and welfare state in which all citizens irrespective of their association with any religious or linguistic combination shall have equal share and opportunity in matters pertaining to education.

The question now arises as to what extent the protection provided by the constitution has improved the educational backwardness of the Muslims. The foregoing paras of this chapter have made it clear that there has been no significant improvement in this respect. It has been rightly pointed out, that adoption of these rights, howsoever hopefully incorporated in the constitution cannot itself be a safeguard unless the rights are given meaning and significant by the courts in whom has the constitution trusted its faith and in whom is confided the power of enforcement.

The noble ideals enshrined in the constitution have not been impelemented in the spirit in which they were incorporated in the constitution. In the New National Policy on Education, 1986,[12] it has been rightly pointed out that the implementation of the constitutional guarantees has been uneven although the various Conferences of Education Ministers, Government of India Memorandum of 1956 as also the statement on languages in 1958 etc. have been laying emphasis on the special treatment to linguistic minorities.

The New Education Policy provides that special efforts need to be taken to bring educationally backward minorities at par with the rest of the society and to make them participate fully in national development activities. It further provides that greater attention will be paid to the education of educationally backward minority groups. This will be of course in the interest of equality and social justice and will naturally include the constitutional guarantees given to them to establish and administer their own educational institutions. Simultaneously, objectivity will be reflected in the preparation of text books and all the school activities, and all possible measures will be taken to promote an integration based on appreciation of common national goals and ideals in conformity with the core curriculum.[13]

In the New Education Policy various programmes have been devised for the educational upliftment of the backward minority groups. The programmes with the supportive funding are intended to be extended during the remaining years of the Seventh Plan. The NCERT, Ministry of Welfare and the Department of Education have taken up the matter with the Vice-Chancellors of Aligarh Muslim University, Marathwada University, Osmania University, University of Kashmir and Jamia Millia Islamia, for setting up Resource Centres which would provide training and guidance to minority educational institutions situated near these centres. The scheme of community Polytechnics as envisaged in the New Education Policy, would also be extended to include five more polytechnics in the minority concentrated areas during the Seventh Plan period.[14] It is believed that the measures envisaged under the New Education Policy will help the educationally backward minority groups to have the maximum possible access to education.

Conclusion

Muslim education in India right from the first Muslim ruler Mohammad Ghori to the last Mughal king has undergone many changes and modifications. All the Muslim kings contributed towards Muslim education. The teachers were respected and education of the masses was given preference. In the period of Mughal king Akbar, the secular education was also introduced with religious education. Every Muslim regime gave a new shape to the Muslim education in India and thereby contributed towards its improvement. The old Madrasas were maintained and new Madrasas were constructed and their standard was raised from time to time. These Madrasas emerged in the form of well established institutions and some of them took the shape of centres of excellence.

The Britishers were interested to introduce their own education system, consequently in the British era, a serious set-back was caused to the Muslim education. The Muslims kept themselves aloof from the English education system and thereby earned the educational backwardness. The Britishers were fully conscious about the consequences of the educational backwardness and they, therefore, took various measures for education of the Muslims. The partition of the country, further caused a serious backlash to the Muslim education and it increased the educational backwardness of the Muslims. The Constitution of India provides various provisions for the protection of the minority educational institutions, but such provisions are hardly implemented in their spirit. In the post-independence period no serious attempt has been made to improve the educational backwardness to the Muslims. The Commissions and Committees appointed to look into the education system failed to pay any special attention to this problem. However, it is very recently that a New National Policy on Education has been adopted, wherein various measures have been suggested to help the educationally backward communities.

References

1. Siddiqui, A.A. Syed Ahmad Khan and the Scientific Society, *Aligarh Magazine* 1970-71.
2. Sir Syed Ahmad Khan : Lecture delivered at Lahore, Feb. 3, 1884.
3. Zaidi, U.H. Syed Mahmud as an Educationist. *Aligarh Law Journal*, Vol, V. 1973, p. 319.

4. *Report of the Indian Education Commission*, 1882-83.
5. Cotton, J.S., *Progress of Education in India*, 1892-93.
6. Shartp, H., *Progress of Education in India*, 1907-12.
7. *Progress of Literacy*, UNESCO publication, 1953.
8. Saxena, N.C., Public Employment and Backwardness among Muslims in India, The Administrator, Vol. XXIX, Nos. 1 & 2.
9. *Ibid.*
10. *Ibid.*
11. Seervai, H.M., *Constitutional Law of India*, 1968, p. 507.
12. *National Policy on Education*. Ministry of Human Resources Development, New Delhi, Aug. 1986.
13. *Ibid.*
14. *Ibid.*

APPENDIX B

METHODOLOGY OF TEACHING IN MADRASAS IN INDIA

Methodology of teaching is closely related to the aims and objectives of education as well as the curriculum. Methodology is in fact the means of achieving the objectives of education as enshrined in the curriculum. Here it is intended firstly to clarify the objectives of Islamic education in the background of the essentials of education as visualised in Islam as well as in the light of the responsibilities of the pupils as the citizen of free and democratic India. This is followed by an analytical study of the present courses and the methods of teaching in Islamic institutions, *i.e.* the Madrasa. Lastly suggestions for improvement have been made so as to help in achieving the objectives of Islamic education in modern India.

I. Objectives in terms of the teaching of Islam

Knowledge is a prerequisite of the understanding of religion as well as the world at large. Emphasis on learning is to be found in the Quran as well as Hadees. The object is to acquaint the Muslims with the mysteries of universe and to help them think over the greatness of God. The Islamic system of education is essentially democratic in spirit as it does not differentiate between man and man on the basis of colour, caste or satus. The Islamic concept of education is flexible and dynamic as well. A peculiar thing about Islam is that it strikes a balance between the material and spiritual values of life. Islam points out that the ideal Muslim is one who does not shun material life but one who lives the world without disturbing the spiritual responsibilities. Islam on the one hand emphasizes basic beliefs and on the other hand tries to develop moral and social qualities. It is generally believed that Islam is against science but this is wrong because Islam lays great stress on observations and thinking and exports the Muslims to master the forces of nature which have been created by God for the benefit of man. There are innumerable references to this in the Quran, pointing out that the manifestations of nature are a challenge to the ingenuity of man for making better uses of these forces such as the sun, the moon, the mountains and the seas, the change of season etc. In this acquisition of scientific knowledge is part and parcel of Islamic education and at par with the acquisition of knowledge of basic beliefs and tenets of Islam. Is it not an irony that Islamic education has been tilted towards theoretical religion at the expanse of scienccs.?

II. Historical Perspective

In the early period of Islamic history particularly upon the tenth century in Baghdad, Damascus, Cairo and Cordova education was both religious and secular in character. It was at a later stage that heretical ideas of the philosophers under the influence of Greek philosophers posed a threat to the Islamic ideology. It was under these conditions that religious leaders felt the need of re-orienting the educational activity in the Islamic world in such a manner as to preserve the essential Islamic ideology and cleansing the body politic of Islam of all heresies and un-Islamic ways of life that had infiltrated into it during the past few centuries. In Baghdad the education system was re-organised by Nizamuddin Tusi which soon spread throughout the length and breadth of the Islamic world. The re-organised institution laid great stress on religious studies as well as Greek logic and philosophy based on deductive reasoning. A parallel to this situation is to be found medieval Europe where the deductive and syllogistic logic of Aristotle was employed for reconciling the main religious values of the church with secular interest. The gigantic literature that developed as a result of the wordy duel between the churchman and the secularists is generally known as scholasticism. It may said that the foundation of Muslim scholasticism was laid during this period. In Islam this work was being done by

Imam Ghazzali. Besides propounding a new theory of Islamic education he classified learning into two kinds—the worthy sciences and the unworthy sciences. He includes religious learning in the first category the learning of which was incumbent on every Muslim. Agriculture medicine and other secular sciences were placed in the second category the learning of which depended on the will of the people. It is obvious that such ideas resulted in the emphasis on religious learning and the neglect of secular learning. Here it may be pointed out that scholasticism in Europe held sway for about two hundred years. It was dethroned from the high pedastal it occupied by the ushering in of Renaissance and the consequent development of natural sciences and the reduction of the power of the church as a whole. The schools of theology were turned into centres of secular learning *e.g.* Paris University grew out of a theological centre of learning. The Islamic scholasticism, however, still continues throughout the Madrasa system. A question here arises as to why Islam has not produced a renaissance although Europe produced it despite scholasticism and persecution of scholars of secular learning. However this does not concerns us here. (This point is discussed in the last chapter of the book.)

III. Needs and Demands of Modern India

The needs and demands of the modern Indian society should also be given due consideration while determining the objectives, curriculum and methodology of teaching in Muslim institutions. Most important need of modern India is to produce intelligent citizens who can shoulder the responsibilities of democratic institutlons. Citizenship in a democracy is very exacting and challenging responsibility for which every citizen has to be trained. To be effective, a democratic citizen one should have the understanding and intellectual capability to sift truth from falsehood, facts from propaganda and to reject dangerous appeals of fanaticism and prejudice. He must develop a scientific mind and should think objectively and should be receptive of new ideas.

If this is the demand of modern India there can be no doubt that the existing curricula of Muslim institution are heavily inclined towards imparting of religious knowledge and the study of the intricacies of logic, grammar and philosophy. Our curriculum is to be enriched and should include the study of secular subjects as practised in the early centuries of Islam. Further, we should not ignore the fact that the pupils from these institutions after finishing their education have to enter life as earning member of society and must get a status equal to those who get education in other schools. The broad basing of the curriculum of the Islamic institution is a prerequisite for the improvement of the methodology of teaching as there will be greater possibility of the use of inductive method of teaching which is conducive to scientific enquiries and experimentation which can hardly be applied to speculative and spiritualistic studies taught at present.

Methods of teaching prevalent in Islamic Institution

The methods of teaching and testing have their roots in the medieval past as pointed out in the main book. They comprise the following types :

1. The text is read by the pupils and its difficulties are explained by the teacher. Some teachers ask the pupils to read the text and they explain the difficulties.
2. Some teachers delivered lectures covering all the aspects given in the text, the pupils generally write down what the teacher spoke, this is called 'Imla'. This method is practised in higher branches of learning.
3. For smaller children the emphasis is on rote learning.
4. In case of advanced studies some teachers lay emphasis on discussion between teacher and taught on the points raised in the text.
5. Sometimes in advanced courses the teachers asks the brilliant students to repeat the lesson imparted by the teacher before the class. This is a sort of training of the pupil for the teaching profession. There are many good features of their methodology of teaching but some of its defects are due to the defective curriculum. As the books prescribed generally pertained to vague

matters so the intellectual exercises are related to vague disputations such as is found the large number of works pertaining to ma'qulāt such as logic, philosophy, dialectics, scholastic literature etc. This results in utter confusion in the minds of the pupils. Instead of promoting clarity of thought they have to comprehend confusing and irrelevant ideas. The remedy lies in making the syllabi more realistic and related to the immediate problems facing the pupils and the society by prescribing modern knowledge side by side with essentials of religious knowledge.

Some of its glaring defects of the method of teaching are as follows :

1. The natural principles are being ignored and the subject is forced on the pupils. They are stuffed with knowledge which they are expected to learn. This state of affairs kills initiative and thinking powers and makes them dull.
2. No consideration is given to proper graduation and articulation of subject matter. It is therefore suggested that abilities and capabilities of the pupils should be given due consideration. The conditions continued upto the nineteenth century when some rethinking was done in institutions like those of Aligarh, Nadwa and Deoband. Aligarh grew into a purely secular institution while Deoband stuck to the old pattern and Nadwa adopted a middle of the course policy, although strictly speaking it too was on the old pattern.

IV. Suggested Method of Teaching

The method of teaching at the higher level is quite satisfactory but at the elementary level a lot of improvement is needed. It should be based on the finding about the learning process. The first principle is that the aptitudes, inclinations and the needs and interest of the pupils should be given due consideration. Secondly there should be fullest opportunity for the play of intellectual powers. Thirdly ample opportunities should be given for the active participation of the pupils in the teaching-learning situations. For this purpose Herbert suggested certain steps of teaching which have long been incorporated in the modern methodology of teaching. These steps are : clearness, association, system and method. Clearness is ensured by creating interest in the subject and by associating new knowledge with the knowledge already possessed by the pupils. Then the pupils are helped to draw generalisation from the mass of information obtained with the help of the teachers and the pupils through talk and discussion and lastly the generalisation are applied in new situations to test their validity. In this way the pupils learn with a deeper understanding of the subject matter. Although this is long and painstaking procedure but it has got to be introduced in our Islamic schools in place of the rote learning method and the book centred education current nowadays. Our teachers generally follow deductive method although Aristotle's inductive method is not unknown to them.

By way of conclusion it may be said that the pupils of the Muslim institutions have long been treated as adults and not as children or adolescents. The teacher and the book has been the pivot of education and the students a non-entity. The result is dampending of the intellectual faculties and killing of initiative and enterprise. No consideration is given to pupil's interests and capacities. Recent attempts at adding a few subject to the already over-loaded and antiquated syllabus are far from satisfactory from the viewpoint of methodology of teaching. The whole set up—aims, curriculum and method—needs revolutionary changes.

BIBLIOGRAPHY

Books (Secondary Sources)

Abdul Haq, *Ethical Philosophy of Ibn Miskawaih*, Aligarh.

——, *Moral Philosophy of Al-Farabi*, Aligarh.

Al-Afendi, M.H., (editor), *Curriculum and Teacher Education*. London, 1980.

Al-Naquib, (editor), al-Attas, S.M., *Aims and Objectives of Islamic Education*, London, 1979.

Ahmad M., *Muslim Education and Scholars*, Zurich, 1968.

Brown, E.G., *A Literary History of Persia*, 4. Volumes. London, 1902-24.

De, Boer, *History of Philosophy in Islam*, London, 1903.

Dodge, *Muslim Education in Medieval Times*, Washington, 1962.

Enan, M.A., *Ibn Khaldūn—his Life and Works*, Lahore, 1944.

Gardener, *An Account of al-Ghazzālī's Life and Works*. Madras, 1919.

Ghafoor A., *Some Aspects of Islamic Education*, Lahore, 1961.

Haymond R., *Philosophy and It's Influence on Medieval Thought*. New York, 1947.

Hitti, *History of the Arabs*, London, 1937.

Hourani, F., *On Harmony of Religion and Philosophy*, London, 1961.

Khan, M. Sharif, *Islamic Education*, Delhi, 1986.

Nadwi, Syed Sulaiman, *Islamic Nizam-i-T'alīm* (Urdu), Azamgarh, 1938.

Nicholson, *Literary History of Arabs*, Chmbridge, 1930.

Ottaway, *Education and Society*, London, 1962.

Quraishi, M.A., *Muslim Education and Learning in Gujarat*, Baroda, 1970.

Shalaby, *A History of Muslim Education*, Beirut, 1954.

Shariff, M.M., *A History of Muslim Philosophy* (in two volumes), Wiesbaden, 1963.

Talal, Khalil, *Contribution of Arabs to Education*, New York, 1926.

Tritton, A.S., *Materials on Muslim Education in the Middle Ages*, London, 1957.

Umaruddın, *Ethical Philosophy of al-Ghazzālī*, Aligarh, 1962.

Watt, W.M., *Muslim Intellectuals—A Study of al-Ghazzālī*, Edenberg, 1963.

Books (Original Sources)

Al-Ghazzālī, *Ihya 'Ulūm al-dīn*, Egypt 1933. English Translation by Fazlul Karim, 4 parts, Delhi, 1982.

Al-Zarnujī, *Ta'līm al-Muta'llim Tarīq al-Ta'llum*. English Translation, Grunebaum, New York, 1958. Urdu Translation by Imitiaz Ali 'Arshī from MS at Raza Library, Rampur, Published in Lahore in *Maqālāt Ar'shī*.

Ibn Khaldūn, *Muqaddima* (*Prolegomena*), English translation by Rosenthal (Three Vols.), Beirut, 1966.

Ibn Miskawaih, *Tahdhīb al-Akhlāq*, Beirut, 1966. English translation by S.K. Zurayak entitled *Refinement of Character*, Beirut, 1968.

Articles

Dar, M.I., Al-Ghazzālī on Problems of Education, *Shafi Presentation Volume* 1955, pp. 33-40.

Fox, A.E., Islam and Modern Education, *Muslim World*, 23 (1933), pp. 29-31.

Goldziher, I., Education (Muslim), *Encyclopaedia of Religion and Ethics*, 1927.

Hamidullah, M., Educational System in the Times of Prophet *Islamic Culture*, 13 (1939), pp. 48-59.

Jaffer, S.M., Islamic Education, *Shafi Presentation Volume*, 1955, pp. 119-129.

Khan, Abdul Muid, Muslim Theories of Education During Middle Ages, *Islamic Culture*, 18, 1944. pp. 418-33.

Khan, Yusuf Husain, The Educational System in Medieval India, *Islamic Culture*, 30, 1956, pp. 106-125.

Khuda Bux, Educational System of the Muslims in the Middle Ages, *Islamic Culture*, 1927, pp. 442-72.

Muzaffaruddin, Some Aspects of Muslim Thought, *Islamic Culture*, 4, 1930, pp. 452-473.

Nadvi, Syed Sulaiman, Islamic and Greek Schools of Philosophy. *Islamic Culture*, I, 1927, pp. 85-91.

Pederson, Some Aspects of the History of Madrasa, *Islamic Culture*, 3, 1929, pp. 525-537.

Picthal, Muslim Education, *Islamic Culture*, 1927, pp. 100-10.

Putney, E.W., Muslim Philosophy of Education, *Muslim World*, 1916, 6, pp. 189-94.

Quraishi, M.A., Educational Ideas of Ibn Khaldūn, *Journal of the M.S. University of Baroda*, 1965, 14, pp. 83-90.

——, Al-Ghazzālī's Philosophy of Education, *Journal of M.S. University of Baroda*, 1964, pp. 63-69.

——, Muslim Teachers and Students in Middle Ages, *Journal of the M.S. University of Baroda*, 1976, 16, pp. 21-38.

Rahman, S.M., Al-Ghazzālī, *Islamic Culture*, I. 1927, pp. 406-11.

Sadiq, I., Avicehna on Education, *Indo-Iranica*, 1956, 9 (4), pp. 71-76.

Seeman, Education in Islam from Jāhiliyya to Ibn Khaldūn, *Muslim World* 1968, 56, pp. 188-98.

Siddiqui, B.H., Ibn Miskawaih's Theory of Education, *Iqbal Review*, 1962, 11, pp. 39-46.

——, The views of Ibn Miskawaih on Education of Children, *Journal of Regional and Cultural Institutions*, 4 (1971), pp. 49-56.

Taufiq, M.A., A Sketch of the Idea of Education in Islam, *Islamic Culture*, I, 1927, pp. 317-327.

Tibawi, A.L., Philosophy of Muslim Education, *Islamic Quarterly*, 1959, pp. 55-60.

——, Muslim Education in the Golden Age of Caliphate, *Islamic Culture*, 1954, 28, pp. 418-38.

Tritton A.S., Arab Theories of Education, *Journal Indian History*, 1925, 3 (3) 4 (1), pp. 35-40.

——, Muslim Education in the Middle Ages, *Muslim World*, 1953, (43), pp. 82-94.

Reference Books

Encyclopaedia of Islam, 1908-38, Under Masjid Sarton, *Introduction to the History of Science*, 3 Volumes, Baltimore, 1927-48.

Hajī Khalīfa, *Kash al-Zunun.*

al-Jāṇiẓ, *Al-Bayān.*

Yāqūt, *Udaba.*

INDEX